THE
FIGHT

ALSO BY DAN BONGINO

Life Inside the Bubble

THE FIGHT

A Secret Service Agent's

Inside Account of Security Failings

and the Political Machine

DAN BONGINO

St. Martin's Press
New York

This book is dedicated to my wife, Paula, and my daughters Isabel and Amelia. Your love and support have made every day a gift, and every moment the beginning of a new adventure.

This is a true story, though some names and details have been changed.

www.stmartins.com

LIBRARY OF CONGRESS CATALOGING-IN-PUBLICATION DATA

Names: Bongino, Dan, author.
Title: The fight : a Secret Service agent's inside account of security failings and the political machine / Dan Bongino.
Description: New York : St. Martin's Press, [2016]
Identifiers: LCCN 2015037098| ISBN 9781250082985 (hardcover) | ISBN 9781250082992 (e-book)
Subjects: LCSH: Bongino, Dan. | United States. Secret Service—Officials and employees—Biography. | National security—United States. | United States—Politics and government—2009– | Washington (D.C.)—Politics and government.
Classification: LCC HV7911.B65 A3 2016 | DDC 320.520973—dc23
LC record available at http://lccn.loc.gov/2015037098

Our books may be purchased in bulk for promotional, educational, or business use. Please contact your local bookseller or the Macmillan Corporate and Premium Sales Department at (800) 221-7945, extension 5442, or by e-mail at MacmillanSpecialMarkets@macmillan.com.

First Edition: January 2016

10 9 8 7 6 5 4 3 2 1

CONTENTS

ACKNOWLEDGMENTS

I f one's life is measured by the impact that they have had on the lives of others, then the value of the lives of the people I want to acknowledge here are immeasurable. My wife Paula grew up on the tough streets of Cali, Colombia, and came to the United States as a child. She overcame a series of obstacles, which have broken the souls of many others, and became a successful business woman, an incredibly dedicated mother, and an inspiration to me during those times where I questioned everything. This book is dedicated to Paula and to my two daughters, Isabel and Amelia, because, without their love and support, there would be no story to tell and no passion to tell it with.

I would also like to thank Senator Mike Lee, Senator Rand Paul, former Alaska governor Sarah Palin, Congressman Louie Gohmert, and former Congressman Allen West for believing in me when I needed support in my fight for a better tomorrow. There are some good men and women left in politics and these individuals are proof of that.

Thank you to Sean Hannity, and to Lynda, Lauren, and Jason,

from the Sean Hannity radio show team, for making this story, and this book possible. Lynda selflessly returned our call and lent a hand when we needed a break, and Lynda and Lauren always seemed to know when I needed a supportive message during a stressful time. And thank you Sean for giving me a chance to be heard by millions on your show. Thank you to Mark Levin and Rich from the Mark Levin radio show for constantly supporting me and being there for me when I needed it. Mark is a true believer in the cause and his passion serves as a daily reminder of what's at stake in this fight. Thank you to Glenn Beck for being a friend when I needed careful advice on how to best fight the good fight. It was your show covering Hayek that motivated me to change direction.

Finally, I would like to thank my campaign team led by Sharon Strine, Maria Pycha, Ally McMahon, Phil Reboli, Jan Schultz, Jerry DeWolf, and Diana Umstot. They refused to quit when the odds were stacked against us, and organized the many dedicated volunteers who selflessly gave their time and energy to join the fight. Dave, Ric, Jeff, Sara, Skip, Kat, Bob, Lisa, Jon, Josh, Missy, Eric, Mary Jane, Sean, Leigh, Dylan, Betsy, and to the many others who helped, I will never forget your efforts.

AUTHOR'S NOTE

W hy should I care about what a former Secret Service agent and former political candidate has to say about governing, leadership, or anything else?" If you picked up this book out of curiosity and are asking yourself that question, then I understand. I understand your hesitancy because I am a born skeptic with a penchant for questioning nearly everything. My first car was a white Ford Escort and the first bumper sticker I placed on that car read, "Question Authority." As you read the book, I ask that you never relinquish your skepticism and that you remember why I chose to write this book. I chose to write the book because some of the best sports coaches were not the most naturally gifted players. Many of these talented and creative coaches were mediocre players who overcame poor genetics, a lack of access to the best training resources, and even poor nutrition and family circumstances, to make it onto the stage with the most elite athletes in the world. They may not have been the star of the team. They may not have been chosen for the lead role in the play. They may not have been chosen as the solo vocalist in the choir. But they overcame a host of challenges and difficulties, and worked their minds and bodies to their limits to earn their spot on that stage.

Growing up at the lower end of the middle class, in a small apartment, above my grandfather's bar on Myrtle Avenue in Queens, New York, I never envisioned a future where I would be a Secret Service agent standing next to the President of the United States and being responsible for ensuring that he is never harmed. I never envisioned becoming the Republican Party's nominee for the U.S. Senate, or running for the U.S. Congress as a largely unknown Republican, in a strongly Democratic state and district, against one of the wealthiest and most popular members of Congress, and coming within one point of defeating him. But I didn't defeat him. I lost. That loss hurt deeply, but I made it on that stage and after leaving that stage I began to think about the path that led me there and how my failures could assist others in getting to that same stage. Maybe some of the lessons I learned will help them become the soloist in the choir that I never was.

I questioned everything after that tough political loss, but after a long period of introspection I found the elusive answer I had sought. Life's journey is a complicated one with a number of twists and turns, some in your control and some not and I had mistakenly believed that the outcome of my journey, not the journey itself, was all that mattered. My political loss, along with many of my experiences as a Secret Service special agent, were a reflection of a deeper truth, which cannot be distilled down to the result of my effort. I realized after the devastating political loss that the result is important, but it is the fight that really matters. Life's challenges are a series of fights and the effort you choose to put into them. Some of these fights will be in vain and some will result in tremendous successes, but the character you build and your individual willingness to sacrifice for "the team" (a concept I will discuss in-depth later in the book) is what you will be remembered for. The legacy you leave others with is not simply the result of your work, but the invaluable lessons you can teach others by the simple act of pouring all of your efforts and energy into a cause you believe in. The result of your efforts, whether it be an election victory in politics, a successful Secret Service security advance, or a completed work project, may have provided you with a deliverable to your fellow man that has marginally improved the world as we know it, but the blood, sweat, and tears that you poured into that effort, regardless of the outcome of it, will be an example to many others who can spread it and cause a chain reaction of hope and optimism.

I wrote *The Fight* to document my successes in the Secret Service and my failures in politics. Both of these experiences provided invaluable templates for a better path forward. The Secret Service, despite some of its recent negative headlines, is a unique operation where special things happen. The special agents I had the honor of serving with didn't care much about the money or the glory; they only cared about the mission. The agents and their families made enormous sacrifices to ensure that the President of the United States was *never* harmed on their watch. How did a government, so associated with models of ineptitude and failure, spawn an agency where the opposite occurs? I'll tell you later in this book. Why is most of our elected government full of people who entered politics for the right reasons, but left without their souls? I'll try to answer that one as well. My hope is that this public airing of my failures and successes will provide some lessons to help you in "the fight" because, in the end, the fight is what really matters.

THE
FIGHT

INTRODUCTION

There Are No Silver Medals in Politics

Win or lose, Republican Dan Bongino has positioned him-self as a rising star in the Maryland GOP with an unex-pectedly close contest against well-heeled incumbent John Delaney."* This was the text that ran underneath a photo of me and my team in *The Baltimore Sun* on November 5, 2014, the day after election day. The congressional campaign my family and I had dedicated our lives to for nearly two years was now over. There were no more doors to be knocked on, get-out-the-vote phone calls to be made, parades or county fairs to attend, or speeches to be given. It was all over. I had left every ounce of spiritual and physical energy I had on the political field of play and, despite running against a well-liked and well-funded incumbent who had defeated an incumbent Republican congressman just two years earlier by over twenty points, in a deep blue state, and being dra-matically outspent, the race was so close that it was going to be

---

*"Winners: Dan Bongino," Editorial, *Baltimore Sun*, November 5, 2014, www
.baltimoresun.com/news/opinion/editorial/bal-bs-ed-wl-bongino-20141022-photo
.html.

decided by the absentee ballot count over the course of the following days.

Just a few hours earlier, as the clock ticked past the midnight hour, I was tearing up while looking at my wife, Paula, my father, and my mother-in-law, as they joined me in the buzzing hotel conference room we had rented as a campaign night war room. I was overwhelmed by emotion as I was closing in on a dramatic political upset that absolutely no one saw coming. Among the sea of pats on the back from excited supporters and the volunteers glued to computer screens as they anxiously hit the ENTER button on their computers to refresh the Maryland State Board of Elections results page, was my wife, Paula, standing over me as I sat in front of the computer that had just displayed us in the lead by thousands of votes. Thinking that the lead I had taken was nearly insurmountable at this point, with more than 90 percent of the polling precincts reporting results, even the skeptics in the room began to believe that the impossible may happen. Seeing the incredible sense of pride in my father's eyes and in the eyes of my mother-in-law, who had come to this country from Colombia decades ago with nothing but a dream in her pocket, as we closed in on a victory in the race for Congress in Maryland's sixth congressional district, was emotionally too much to take after a long two years of emotional highs and lows, and the tears were difficult to hold back.

Not one mainstream political prognosticator had rated the congressional race I chose to enter into as anything other than "Safe Democratic." When you are the Republican running in that race, this is never a good sign. Compounding the problem was that the local media outlets had ignored our pleas for fair campaign press coverage of the excitement we were generating within the state. The preordained media outcome in the race was so striking that just four days before the election *The Washington Post*'s Arelis Hernandez declared, in the headline of her piece on the larger Maryland political picture, "In Maryland's eight congressional races, incumbents face little competition."* Despite these headwinds pushing against our campaign's sails we executed a well-designed campaign plan that I knew would give us a chance, albeit a small one, at victory.

When the polls closed late in the evening, the Maryland State Board of Elections reported the results of early voting within minutes and the results were devastating. Early voting results in Maryland are a generally reliable indicator of how the election is going to go and Congressman Delaney was ahead by double digits. The look on Paula's face, as she walked back into the room from putting our two-year-old daughter down to sleep in the hotel room and looked at the computer screen, was a mix of breathtaking disappointment and anxiety. She was wondering the same thing I was: "How were we going to tell the hundreds of excited supporters who had gathered in the hotel that we were going to lose badly?" We were both more concerned with their feelings of disappointment than ours because they had all poured their time and energy into the campaign effort. I looked around the room and, as my eyes met the eyes of volunteers and supporters who I had developed personal relationships with as we spent hours knocking on doors and discussing everything from sports to philosophy, it became more and more difficult to disguise my disappointment.

As the early polling precincts began to report their results from the heavily Democratic Washington, DC, suburbs, Congressman

---

*Arelis Hernandez, "In Maryland's eight congressional races, incumbents face little competition," *Washington Post*, October 31, 2014, manty.fsdkff.com/local/md-politics /md-congressional-incumbents-expected-to-win-reelection/2014/10/31/0a36fe3e-5ec5 -11e4-8b9e-2ccdac31a031_story.html.

Delaney's lead grew and I began to worry that all of the more than seven thousand doors I had personally knocked on during the campaign had amounted to nothing. Were the political prognosticators correct and had I grossly misjudged my ability to politically persuade people? I knew that the race was a formidable political hill to climb, but I didn't expect a double-digit loss and wasn't even prepared to deliver a concession speech under those circumstances. I penciled a few notes on a napkin nearby and they all followed the same theme: how sorry I was for letting everyone down. Ironically, as Paula looked at me and quietly said, "All that work, and we're left with this," more results came in from the western and mountain portions of the district and that double-digit lead began to drop. Hours had now passed and the excitement in the packed war room began to grow. We had rented a number of rooms in the hotel for the event—a conference room with some food, a room for my family, and a small ballroom decorated appropriately for either a concession or victory speech—but everyone was packed tightly into the small war room and the hallway outside looking both into the room and over computers and the volunteers' shoulders for updated results.

At around eleven o'clock at night it happened, although I was skeptical. My friend Brian Terriberry, who had accompanied me throughout the day, forcefully poked me on my shoulder and shoved his cell in my face. On his screen was an Associated Press elections tracker that showed me in the lead by two points. When I looked around the small room and hallway and noticed that hundreds of people were staring at device screens hitting the REFRESH button, all on the same wireless connection, it all made sense. Brian's smartphone must have been the first device to get the new results and the other computers, including mine were slow to catch up due to the heavy Web traffic. At this point, it began to sink in that we had taken the lead in the race. The mixed martial arts practitioner in me burst out, and in a fit of joy I punched down on the table in front of me in pure joy. Everyone in the room looked surprised and confused, wondering if this was rage or joy. When I screamed, "We're winning," the mood turned instantly from nervous anxiety to a blanket of joy so thick with pent-up emotion that you could almost touch it. My Twitter account began to overflow with well-wishes from supporters and astonishment from political insiders who couldn't believe that we were ahead in a race they had all written off as unwinnable for me. One of the more humorous tweets I saw, from an account using the handle @EsotericCD read: "I seriously don't understand how it's possible that Dan Bongino (R) is beating John Delaney (D) in MD06. And yet it's happening. #crazypills."

At 12:30 a.m., with 86 percent of the votes in, and my lead at just under 3 percent, I grabbed my campaign manager, Sharon, and said to her, "If we pull this off, I need five minutes." I wanted to be sure that after my wife and I had an opportunity to digest this moment that I didn't forget the architect and engineer of the campaign plan that was making this race a nail-biter, against all the odds. I then grabbed my wife, who was standing to the left of the seat I hadn't left in hours and tightly grabbed her around the waist. It was her innumerable sacrifices that had made that moment possible however fleeting it turned out to be in the end. No one ever prepares the spouses of political candidates for the rigors of a hard-fought campaign and she had never left my side. Although I was overjoyed and new rounds of eye contact with supporters were met by tears and smiles from ear to ear, I noticed that Dylan and Leigh from my campaign team, who had been huddled next to me the entire night doing the tedious electoral math, were not sharing in the moment. Dylan let me enjoy the next few glances and smiles, but then told me the troubling news. He said that the few remaining polling precincts left were largely from the heavily Democratic portions of the district and he wasn't sure that our lead would hold. The minutes passed excruciatingly slowly as the final votes arrived at the State Board of Elections and were input into the system for the world to see. As those minutes passed and Dylan, Leigh, and I scrambled to calculate the voting math, the results came in before the pencils could process the calculations. We had an erasable SMART Board behind me, which we constantly updated. Phil and Sara, from my campaign team, stole glances at my computer from over my shoulder and updated it from us leading by two thousand votes, to up by a couple of hundred votes, to up by seventy-one votes, to down by seventy-one votes, to down by a couple of hundred votes before the stream of incoming results slowed down. Paula and I were crushed and everyone in the room knew it. It was as if a super-powered emotional vacuum had just sucked all of the positive energy out of the room. The foil of being overcome with joy at our unexpected potential victory and then in minutes having it all ripped away as the final few polling precincts came in, made the experience far worse. I knew there were thousands of absentee and provisional ballots outstanding and if the vote deficit remained within a few hundred votes, we still had a great chance at victory. But as the final precincts came in, we fell behind by a slim thousand-plus votes. The only question remaining, after the most draining emotional roller-coaster ride I had been on since my days in hot zones in the Secret Service, was: "Were there enough outstanding absentee votes from the heavily Republican portions of the district to catch up?"

I owed my supporters who had been packed into that small, hot room for most of the night an update. They had watched me sitting in that chair for hours smiling, crying, laughing, frowning, joyous, angry, frustrated, and finally beaten, and they were owed an explanation. I thanked them profusely and told them it was not going to be decided tonight and that it was probably best that we all went home and prepared for an absentee ballot count, which could take days. I couldn't escape the thought that the emotionally drained and ill version of me that they were seeing would be the last image of me that would be with them. It's still this memory of that night that haunts me the most.

Over the next few days I realized the race was over and that the absentee vote count was never going to be enough to overcome now reelected Congressman Delaney's lead. I genuinely liked the congressman and we had a pleasant conversation on the phone where we both knew that the time for a concession was rapidly arriving. The conversation was made easier by the fact that, although I had been the unwitting star of his barrage of negative campaign commercials for weeks, and was going to lose an unexpectedly tight race at the last moments to him, I thought he was a genuinely good person.

"What could have been?" This is possibly the most painful question anyone can ask upon self-reflection. Looking back on the campaign and the final result is still painful for my wife and me as we both, whether we openly acknowledge it or not, ask that question often. What if we both hadn't been terribly sick for the final two weeks of the campaign? What if we had just raised a bit more money? What if the local media hadn't constantly told Maryland voters that the race was "uncompetitive"? What if the national Republican Party had backed our efforts? When you fall short in

any effort, which you passionately believe in, you can "what if?"
yourself into the middle of a circular firing squad, and it took me
some time to stop playing this dangerous game. There are no silver
medals in politics and I lost. I've accepted that, and this book is my
effort to try and generate a positive outcome from a painful event.
All of the "what ifs" and the lessons I have learned during my experiences as a police officer, Secret Service agent, and candidate
for elected office are the headings of the chapters of *The Fight* and
within each chapter I've used personal stories of my experiences as
a New York City police officer on the tough streets of East New
York, Brooklyn, as a Secret Service agent inside the DC "bubble,"
and as a political candidate, to provide concrete, real-world
examples. Although my campaign manager and my campaign
team designed an incredible strategy, which nearly transformed a
universally declared unwinnable race into the congressional upset
of the 2014 election cycle, "almost" only counts in horseshoes and
hand grenades. The lessons I learned and then how to apply them
to a fractured political system were difficult to recount, but maybe
there is some nobility in cutting a trail for others to walk on. You
decide.

1

The White House Fence Jumper

It was a Friday night and I just sat down at my kitchen table after a long day of campaigning. After knocking on approximately a hundred doors, I took my daughter to her swimming class, returned home with her, and, as I typically did when I had a free moment, I glanced down at my Twitter account to see what was going on in the world. I immediately noticed a strange tweet directed to me from a producer at CNN, asking me about a fence-jumping incident at the White House. I hadn't heard anything about the incident because I was driving with my daughter just minutes prior, but I didn't think there was much of a story there because no one else was e-mailing or calling me from the media about it. Whenever incidents had happened relating to the Secret Service, my cell phone and e-mail account would erupt with media requests and, absent the tweet, I hadn't heard from anyone and figured it was a minor story on a slow news night. After the incident with the Secret Service in Cartagena, Colombia, I was accustomed to media "pile-ons," but the media firestorm White House fence jumper Omar Gonzalez initiated was unlike anything I had lived through in the past as this story grew geometrically and eventually led to the downfall of most of the Secret Service's upper-level management. The lesson we can all take away from this incident is that, sometimes, even the Secret Service takes security for granted and in this new era of global terrorism, threat assessment and management, and the prevalence of soft targets, security is probably an afterthought at your workplace as well.

I, along with many of my former Secret Service colleagues, saw the security failures of September 19, 2014 (the date of the fence-jumping incident), coming. We all wished away the threat and hoped that the clearly inadequate security fence surrounding the White House would one day be replaced with a barrier adequate enough to separate the President of the United States from the legions of serious threats to his life roaming around the exterior of the White House grounds. There are a number of visually impressive centers of power in Washington, DC, ranging from the Capitol building to the Supreme Court, but there are few magnets for the attention of psychopathological assassins like the White House. When I served as an agent in the New York Field Office's protective intelligence section, the division that investigates presidential threat cases that comes to our attention, I was consistently amazed at the creativity displayed in the minds of potential assassins with regard to the reasons they were targeting the President or the White House. While reading some of their letters or during our interviews with these subjects, they would state reasons ranging from, "they're hiding aliens in the White House" to "the President stole my girlfriend." Many of these clearly disturbed men and women had never had contact with the mental health system and I viewed my role in the protective intelligence section as more of a social worker one than a law enforcement one. It is shocking how so many of

these deeply disturbed people live alternate lives of sincere para-
noia and psychological distress, yet function almost normally in
other portions of their lives and, therefore, they avoid detection
while walking among us.

One particular case stands out to me as an example of this phe-
nomenon; I will call him Joe to preserve his anonymity. Joe came
to my attention through a series of threatening letters he authored,
which were written to people under the protection of the Secret Service and they all had the warning signs of a potentially dangerous
threat case. One of those warning signs, that may seem counterintuitive to the casual observer, is target shifting. When a psychologically disturbed individual threatens or shows an unusual
interest in a number of different targets (i.e., politicians, celebrities,
sports figures) and isn't focused on one specific person, that is a
historical indicator of an elevated threat based on the thousands
of interviews the Secret Service has conducted in their extensive
research on threat assessment. Films, such as *In the Line of Fire*
starring Clint Eastwood, which tells the story of a singular obsession with the assassination of the President by an assassin played
by John Malkovich, give the impression that the most dangerous
potential assassins are those that are laser focused on one target.
But the Secret Service's internal research and experience points to
the opposite conclusion. Those who promiscuously target numerous
people with their pathological thoughts and desires are far more
dangerous. A potent example is the attempted assassination of
President Ronald Reagan by John Hinckley. Hinckley was motivated not by an obsession with Reagan (Hinckley actually targeted President Jimmy Carter before settling on Reagan), but by a
desire to impress actress Jodie Foster who he had grown pathologi-
cally attached to.

When I first read "Joe's" letters, his target shifting, and the detail by which he laid out exactly what he wanted to do to the various people he was obsessed with, I knew we had a problem. Threats to the President, no matter how seemingly innocuous or grave, are all treated with the same urgency within the Secret Service, but I knew this one was different and that time was not on our side. I did some investigative homework on Joe and through a computer search I found out where he worked. With the permission of the Secret Service office supervisor, who agreed with my evaluation of the threat level of the situation, I immediately grabbed a colleague of mine named "Brad" and sped over to the small grocery store where Joe worked. When we entered the store, one of those old neighborhood grocery stores that the bigger chains have since driven out of business, one of the employees must have sensed immediately who we were looking for. I don't know if he had recently spoken with Joe and sensed that something had gone wrong with him, or if Joe had threatened him, but the employee knew why we were there and pointed toward the deli counter in the back of the store. Oddly enough, neither Brad nor I had displayed our issued Secret Service credentials and I jokingly remarked that the store employee must have thought we were there for a sandwich. The store was small enough that Brad and I could see portions of the deli counter in the rear of the store in between the aisles that broke up the full visual picture. Although we didn't have a photo of Joe, the man we saw pacing back and forth, in and out of view, as he disappeared between the visual obstructions of the grocery shelves in the aisles, was clearly our guy. I looked at Brad and nothing needed to be said as we both knew what the other was thinking as we watched Joe's frantic pacing: "This could get bad." We didn't want to unnecessarily escalate the situation by running toward Joe so we briskly walked the short distance from the front to the rear of the store and the seconds felt like minutes as Joe would disappear and reappear from view, each second appearing more agitated based on his furtive movements. Brad made it to the rear of the store first and when Joe saw Brad he immediately ran to the far corner behind the thick, see-through deli glass case. I could see a distorted image through the glass deli case and I noticed that Joe had grabbed something and was now loudly screaming at us. He was frantic and was demanding to know why we were there, but his body was angled in such a way that it blocked my view of what he was holding. It was then that I heard Brad yell, "Knife!" The Secret Service and the NYPD had trained me in their respective academies that the minimum safe distance from a knife-wielding adversary was twenty-one feet, even with your firearm out and fixed on the adversary (based on the adversary's ability to cover that twenty-one-foot distance in a brief amount of time and inflict fatal stab wounds before a law enforcement officer can properly react). I knew we were in grave danger as Brad was approximately six feet away and was far enough behind the counter that if Joe were to lunge at him he would have difficulty escaping. I drew my firearm desperately trying to train my weapon's sights on Joe but his rapid hand and head movements, as he gestured toward both Brad and then me, with the large butcher knife, prevented me from getting a clear picture through the front sight of my black Secret Service issued P229 Sig Sauer handgun. Making matters far worse, the deli case blocked most of Joe's vital organs making a shot, which would stop Joe, if necessary, nearly impossible (contrary to what some members of the general public believe, police officers and federal agents are trained to shoot only to stop assailants, they are *not* trained to fire their weapons to kill assailants).

Brad, sensing the threat, drew his weapon out and we both screamed at the top of our lungs, "Drop the knife, drop the knife!" When you are in that moment, as many law enforcement officers who have been there can attest to, the only thing you see is that knife and it appears twice as large when it is being directed at you. Although only minutes had passed since we encountered Joe, my brain deceived me into believing that I had spent hours staring at that butcher knife as Joe menacingly waved it through space. A deadly weapon, with your eyes trained on it, is almost hypnotic in its ability to warp time, the possibility of an ugly death will do that to the mind. As employees of the grocery store began to swarm to the rear of the store, and watch in astonishment at what was occurring, Joe began to slow down his frantic hand and head movements. It was only when a store employee screamed that Joe reluctantly dropped the knife on the counter. Strangely, the presence of the store employees seemed to break Joe's out-of-control state of rage and return him to reality from the conspiratorial world his psychologically damaged other half resided in. Brad and I had awoken the "Mr. Hyde" portion of Joe's Dr. Jekyll and Mr. Hyde personality by our mere presence in the store, which seemed to confirm to him all of the bizarre conspiracy theories Joe had written about in the letters he authored, which brought him to the Secret Service's attention.

That incident was the closest I came to a deadly use-of-force scenario as a law enforcement officer and, more than a decade later, I still recall each minor detail. I remember thinking to myself with regard to the grocery store employees who saw the incident, "These are just kids, are they going to have to witness me shooting this man?" These types of incidents are all too frequent occurrences within the Secret Service as they fulfill their mission investigating the many threats to the President of the United States and I wonder if the Secret Service sniper assigned to the White House roof on the day fence jumper Omar Gonzalez scaled the White House fence was thinking the same thing about the kids outside of the White House fence line.

Unfortunately many of the psychologically disturbed men and women that the Secret Service come into contact with in their threat investigations are first encountered, not behind the deli counter of a local supermarket, but on the White House side of the seven-and-a-half-foot tall, black, iron fence separating the secure White House grounds from the unsecure public space. The White House fence, as it appeared on that fateful night that Omar Gonzalez scaled it and made it inside of the East Room of the White House State Floor, has not been significantly altered since 1965. The September 11, 2001, terror attacks, the Oklahoma City bombing, the World Trade Center bombing, and a number of other terror attacks of varying degrees of sophistication all tragically came and went without any significant security upgrades to the fence that separates the President from the many who wish to do him and his family harm. The story of the fence, Gonzalez's scaling of it, and the failure to upgrade it, is a microcosm of the larger problems infecting the Secret Service, our government, and the failure of many of today's businessmen and women to properly account for security in an increasingly dangerous world.

If you were to take a portion of the White House fence, as it existed during the Omar Gonzalez incident, paint it a different color to disguise where it came from, take a picture of it, and show it to a Secret Service agent and ask him if he would secure a low-threat facility with it, he would laugh in your face. The fence we used to secure the Olympic Village at the Winter Olympics in Salt

Lake City, Utah, in 2002 (a facility with a threat profile far less significant than that of the White House) when the Secret Service designed the security plan, was as technologically advanced as any in the world. Using both technologically advanced security measures such as vibration detectors, and simple ones such as a fence high enough to make scaling it, without being detected, nearly impossible; it was well-suited to keeping those who may have wished the Olympic athletes harm, out. The Salt Lake City Olympic Committee had little experience with security, but neither they, nor the Secret Service, were going to allow a repeat of the 1972 Munich Olympics terror attacks where, at 4:00 a.m., eight heavily armed terrorists from the terrorist group Black September scaled a lightly guarded fence separating the Olympic Village from the general public and brutally murdered members of the Israeli Olympic team. There's an old adage that states, "Good fences make good neighbors." If that's true then, at a minimum, good fences make for good security and while designing the Olympic Village security plan, the fence was priority number one.

If the fence was a priority for the Olympic athlete's "home" during the Secret Service's security planning session for the 2002 Olympics, then how did nearly everyone seem to miss the grotesquely inadequate fence "securing" the home of the President of the United States? The answer is: they didn't. The fence fell victim to the very same bureaucratic and political mess that many other intractable policy problems have fallen victim to with the Washington, DC, power brokers; leadership obsessed with the accumulation of power and influence and less concerned with basic problem-solving. Problem-solving within the bureaucratic class in Washington, DC, requires the recognition of a "problem" first and that mandates that a bureaucrat call attention to some policy or procedure that someone else is invested in. This is a risk and risk-takers are shunned within the Washington, DC, bureaucratic class. This is not a problem unique to government, but it is a problem ubiquitous within the public sector. My experience within the Secret Service, a government agency charged with the most grave of responsibilities, securing the life of the President and his family, is that portions of their management were not immune to the trappings of this obsession with power and the avoidance of risk. The temptation in the Secret Service to follow the herd and not "rock the boat" was suffocating at times. The upper-level management answered a number of pressing questions from their workforce with the same answer—"because that's the way we've always done it"—so often, that it became a tragic, ongoing joke among the rank-and-file agents.

The federal government bureaucracy is so thick and layered that the management at the top of agencies such as the Secret Service is insulated from the agents doing the work at the bottom. This layer of insulation provides the incentives for many of the managing members of the organization to maintain the status quo, despite glaring inefficiencies. Whereas innovation and creativity in problem-solving can provide for material and psychological rewards in the private sector—through salary increases, bonuses, and promotions—my experience within government is the polar opposite. The impetus for change and innovation within the government is external, not internal because there is little reward for pointing out errors when serving in management. Those "errors" and mistakes are historical decisions made by other managers within the Secret Service, and publicly exposing them through work channels is a career death sentence if that person discovers that you were the one who sounded the alarm. It's one thing not to be rewarded for trying to fix a problem, but it's something entirely different to be punished for pointing out a problem and proposing a solution for it. My experiences within the federal government, in dealing with a number of managers from different agencies within its infrastructure, have led me to believe that there are limited exceptions to this model.

Overcoming the bureaucratic inertia of government, and implementing a new, and innovative, approach to public-sector inefficiencies, is only brought about by public pressure, and through legislative channels, when failings are exposed in the media. Again, using the Secret Service as an example, it was the assassination of President John F. Kennedy that brought about substantial changes to the way the Secret Service handled motorcade security by altering how we looked at everything from open-top vehicles to sharp turns in the road, which force us to slow the vehicles down. It was the shooting of President Ronald Reagan, which led the Secret Service to eliminate public arrivals and departures and to move toward covered arrival and departure areas (if an assassin can't see the President they'll have a difficult time accurately targeting him). And, sadly, it took the scaling of the White House fence, and a near miss with Omar Gonzalez who was tackled inside the White House just feet from the stairway leading to the residence of the President of the United States, to change the way the Secret Service saw the White House fence.

Compounding the Secret Service's bureaucratic inertia problem was their 2003 transfer from the Department of the Treasury to the massive new Department of Homeland Security. This transfer created a mad scramble for dollars and influence among the agencies both assigned to, and created by, the new Department of Homeland Security and it reinforced the incentive to maintain the

Secret Service's status quo, however dangerous the status quo was becoming. Try to imagine yourself as a member of the upper management of a major corporation, with a billion dollar budget, and thousands of employees, as the Secret Service has, and being absorbed in a hostile takeover by a larger firm where you are entirely unfamiliar with the management and the culture? This is a challenge in the corporate world even with large financial incentives, which are aligned to ensure that the acquisition succeeds. If the stock price of the new, larger firm collapses, or there is an exodus of talented employees due to low morale pursuant to the merger, the stakeholders in the firm would howl in protest and demand change. But what if none of that happened? What if low-morale, principal-agent problems, bureaucratic inefficiencies, angling for access to the new power structure for personal reasons, and general unrest were allowed to fester with no resolution in sight? This question is an accurate synopsis of where the Secret Service found itself after the Department of Homeland Security transfer and the subsequent jockeying afterward. Put yourself in the shoes of the Secret Service director under these circumstances and, using the White House fence example ask yourself, honestly, what would you do given these hypothetical choices?

1. You can make major changes to the clearly inadequate White House fence and, in the process, debate with the White House Staff over the "optics" of the new fence, fight with the Department of Homeland Security overfunding for the new fence, debate with the White House Historical Society over the changes to the property and, in the process use up any goodwill you had with the White House staff (who can destroy your career), and the Department of Homeland Security who will be sure to

marginalize you in the executive branch chain of command for causing a "problem."

2. You can choose to do nothing to the fence because nothing has been done to the fence for fifty years (since no other Secret Service manager has done anything about it in the past), and, through your lack of action, save your career by never having to answer for something you didn't do.

Clearly, you can see how the incentives for managers within the federal government are to do a lot of little things that make you appear busy, but will not put a bull's-eye on your back for being a "troublemaker." Remember, there are no shareholders to answer to as there are in the private sector. You answer to politically connected bureaucrats and White House staff members, with limited, if any, experience in security matters, who never have to face either a shareholder or a voter. As long as you look busy, maintain the status quo, and promote your friends through the agency's management chain (who, not coincidentally, will likely remain behind in the agency after you leave and be able to assist you in your new career as a well-paid security executive in the private sector), you are untouchable. During my time in business school at Penn State University we learned about BHAGs or "Big Hairy Audacious Goals," a tongue-in-cheek way of describing visionary goals. These BHAGs are largely absent within the federal bureaucratic morass because the BHAGs will draw unnecessary attention to any executive within the government promoting them, and that attention will cause someone else to have to admit to a mistake of omission or commission that he or she might have made after your "solution" pointed it out. Do you really believe that the Department of Homeland Security Secretary, who likely has either private-sector champagne wishes or public-sector caviar dreams when pondering his own future, is thinking about why the President lives in a house where the fence couldn't stop a mentally disturbed, out of shape, forty-two-year-old man from nearly entering his residence? Of course not, someone probably told him, it's that way "because that's the way we've always done it" and, sadly, that was good enough.

No one was worried about the obvious security disaster the White House fence presented because no one had been worried about it in the past and "because that's the way we've always done it." It was out of sight and out of mind, even though it was neither for the Secret Service nor for Omar Gonzalez. Big changes within the government do not resemble those in the private sector where restless shareholders watch a company's stock price like hawks. Change within the government resembles a local gathering of chess players who meet at the same time everyday in the public park, and are hostile to any disruption to their schedule. But change in the government does happen and it resembles the evolutionary theory of "punctuated equilibrium" where a species remains static for extended periods with no changes and then some external event causes a rapid and massive scale change where the species is altered forever. Sadly, those external events in the Secret Service, and throughout the government branches I have come into contact with, are usually tragic ones (see the media pressure, which ensued pursuant to the Veterans Health Administration scandal of 2014 where military veterans died waiting for healthcare services). When you trace the major historical changes in the way the Secret Service protects the Presidents you can marry them up with some tragic event. Motorcade security, avoiding convertible, open-top vehicles, and the focus on long-range threats such as snipers began after the assassination of President John F. Kennedy. Covered arrivals either underground or in tents, and the screening of anyone within handgun range of the President happened after the shooting of President Ronald Reagan. The closing of Pennsylvania Avenue, to prevent the destruction of the White House by vehicle-borne explosives, happened after the terror attacks of September 11, 2001. And, the ridiculously substandard White House fence only became an urgent security issue after Omar Gonzalez scaled it and was only a few feet from scaling the steps to the White House residence.

The Secret Service, and the federal government in general, cannot continue to operate this way and the rank-and-file agents will have to be given a credible voice at the table without the fear of career damaging repercussions, in order to repair a broken system missing consistent public accountability. Many of the aforementioned issues were known to the rank-and-file agents beforehand, but if you were the agent to mention to the Secret Service director that the White House fence should be changed on an elevator ride with him in our headquarters building, you would likely be laughed out of the building. Consider a private-sector company that could only tinker with the small problems while the incentives for its executives to keep quiet about the larger ones were set in place? Imagine a company selling a soft drink and tinkering with the bottle cap machine while all the employees knew that the drink in the bottle they are selling tasted terrible? How long do you think the management team would stay in position and the company would stay profitable?

I do not intend to lionize the private sector here, just to present the failures of the public sector using an analogy, which makes it easier to understand. After all, many private-sector companies have also been lost in the minutiae and failed to see the groundswell of change headed their way. Any doubts about this should be redirected to the executives at Myspace and BlackBerry, one of which was driven out of business quickly by a ferocious competitor called Facebook, and another which either never saw the iPhone coming, or severely underestimated the existential threat to its product line. The changes I will recommend in this book are based on experiences I had within the government, which can be applied to both the public and private sector because they are centered on repairing the systemic problems with poorly aligned incentives.

A salary is not an incentive to do anything other than show up for work if the person receiving it isn't tied in some way to a measurable outcome. The federal government is rife with positions where you are paid the same amount whether you are Michael Jordan or Jordan Michael, and if this doesn't change, we will continue to throw taxpayer money down a rathole to create new government problems rather than to solve old ones. Our federal government managers should be rewarded for innovation and for finding efficiencies within the government. The incentives should be for government managers to find ways to garner more output from the same number of employees, or get the same output per employee for less taxpayer inputs. If we allowed these managers to keep some of these cost savings in their respective divisions from reducing inefficiencies, or we rewarded them for the increased output with the same amount of taxpayer input, then this would create an obvious incentive to treat the taxpayer's money as they would their own. To prevent federal government managers from abusing this responsibility and indiscriminately cutting taxpayer money and other inputs from programs that are working well and breaking the backs of the workers to inefficiently save a penny in

nonproductive-enhancing ways, we could make that manager's
position and cash rewards contingent on maintaining a generally
positive recommendation from the employees he or she super-
vises. The employees would submit timely and anonymous evaluations of their supervisors (with outlier evaluations discarded to
prevent personal feelings, positive or negative, from corrupting the
process) and these evaluations would be used to determine if the
managers keep, as a cash reward, the savings the managers have
found in their programs. And, if your company is one of those
that is content with the status quo and where the bottle cap machine is top notch but the drink tastes terrible, you may want to
ask yourself: "How long do I have before someone jumps our company's fence and winds up in our boardroom?"

Of course, security failures as a result of inattention within
sprawling bureaucracies are not limited to the federal government.
In my experience within the security field, security is typically
treated as one would treat a fresh coat of office paint: It looks really nice, but it really doesn't add anything to the company's value
and, in a new era where soft targets are becoming the new normal
with regard to terrorist target selection, this is a dangerous posture.
I'm frequently asked by friends and colleagues, "Is my office safe?"
Sadly, the response is typically, "No." During my time as a special
agent with the Secret Service I saw the internal security workings
of hundreds of hotels, airports, high-rises, universities, expensive
homes, factories, warehouses, and small businesses, and I've rarely
been impressed. They frequently confuse access control (i.e., badges,
security codes, PIN numbers) with viable deterrents. It's armed
deterrents that are the core of a security plan, not security badges.

Terror groups are most assuredly planning a *Charlie Hebdo*
type of assault within the United States as you read this. Contrary

to the opinions of some terrorism experts who claim that these attacks require an extensive degree of planning, I take the opposing position. These small arms tactical attacks on soft targets require that the terrorists learn how to fire their weapons, reload, use explosives, and perform basic surveillance, and these easy-to-develop skills are all that they need to inflict destruction and chaos. Contrast this with the planning that went into the September 11, 2001, attacks, where multiple hijackers had to learn to pilot a large aircraft, smuggle objects onto planes, navigate, and, at the same time, keep operational security tight enough to leave no investigative footprints. If a terror group's end goal is to inspire collective fear and anxiety through their attacks then, if you think as they do, why would they waste the resources, or risk the threat of arrest and interrogation if the very same sick goals could be accomplished with far fewer complications? There's no need to panic and live in fear but there is a need to recognize that the savages we are fighting do not fear death and we must do everything we can, within reason, to "harden up" our soft targets and make the United States, and the White House, as unappealing a target as possible.

2

What Bureaucrats Can Learn
from the Secret Service
Security Model

The debacle with the White House fence and the failure to implement a more modern and secure fix to it, is not indicative of the Secret Service culture as a whole. While the previous chapter focused on some of the failings at the upper-management level of the Secret Service, this chapter is focused on the many things the Secret Service, through the dedicated work of the rank-and-file agents, does better than anyone. There is no comparable public or private entity that has the ability to initiate and prepare a security advance for a high-threat-level world leader in the way the Secret Service does. With as little as a few days' notice, I have witnessed and been a part of, the Secret Service coordinating complicated overseas security missions for the President. Missions, which required us to transport hundreds of men and women from the military, Secret Service and White House staff, along with hundreds of thousands of pounds of weapons, armored vehicles, transport helicopters, communications equipment, chemical and biological detection equipment, motion sensors, and cameras. There are no excuses within the Secret Service and when the White House staff gets the notice from the President's decision makers that he wishes to take a foreign trip then we have to make it happen and ensure it happens safely. I have never heard of a situation during my time with the Secret Service where the security situation on the ground in a country enabled the Secret Service to effectively persuade the President to cancel a dangerous foreign trip. When the President says it is happening, then it is happening. In sharp contrast to this "get it done, no matter what it takes" attitude, I was surprised to learn from a friend of mine, who was a member of a labor union, that he wasn't allowed to start work five minutes early because the union would accuse him of "breaking conditions." He told me that the union viewed this as a violation of their work arrangement with the company and that it was forbidden. If you are looking for a model to ensure mediocrity in the workplace, then punishing those who take initiative is surely a well-worn path there. The model the Secret Service employs is the polar opposite of this and is so successful that, despite thousands of visits by both the President of the United States and world leaders to, and from, the United States, the incidents of serious physical harm or death to these world leaders due to security lapses are so rare that they are memorable to nearly everyone when they happen. This is in no way meant to excuse the security failures that contributed to the assassination of President Kennedy or the shooting of President Reagan (the last chapter covered some of the institutional shortcomings that contributed to these failures), but to show how, even under suboptimal upper management, the culture of the Secret Service has imbued in its agents a work ethic that enables the mission's success, even in the face of management obstacles.

Although some in the Secret Service management chain have failed to promote a culture of innovation in the broader sense (i.e., promotion systems that are based solely on merit, innovation with regard to new weapons systems and physical security technologies), there is a sense of esprit de corps among the men and women of the Secret Service that I've yet to see replicated anywhere else in my journey through the private sector and politics. There's no question that the transfer to the Department of Homeland Security, the devastating prostitution scandal in Cartagena, Colombia, and the many security failures in the fence-jumping incident with Omar Gonzalez, took a heavy toll on Secret Service morale, but the agents I keep in contact with still speak fondly about the Secret Service and they do it with an unmistakable passion when discussing the importance of the protection mission. One of the agents I worked with during my tenure in the agency described his relationship with the Secret Service this way: "It's like my marriage, I complain about it all the time, but if my wife left me, I'd be miserable." When I was conducting security advances I was guilty of some of the same behavior. I would complain about the lack of support from management on a decision I had made during an advance, but I would never let it impact the mission and knew that, in the end, the Secret Service would back me up if I made the right call. That relentless commitment to keeping the President safe and secure, regardless of the time or effort it takes, the mood you're in, the fatigue you're feeling, or the money you're making, is a characteristic of the Secret Service that has no equal.

From the first moments in training to the final moments of a Secret Service agent's career, the devastating reminders of the consequences of failure are everywhere. The agents are acutely aware that, fair or unfair, the Secret Service will largely be defined by its failures and not by its successes. This is an extremely difficult standard to live by but no President, member of the White House staff, or member of the media is going to thank a Secret Service agent for getting the President from point A to point B safely, it's simply expected. But they will punish the Secret Service with questions if the President's motorcade causes a noticeable traffic tie-up in a city we visit. The punishment for even small failures on a security advance is being stigmatized by your peers as someone who just "can't get it done." It's this relentless pressure to never let the agent next to you down that motivates many of the agents I worked with to work through the late nights and to get up early in the morning, whether compensated for it or not, to make sure the security advance is done correctly. I was frequently asked by friends and neighbors if my job as a Secret Service agent was stressful because of the danger, and I would always answer that it wasn't the danger that was stressful, but it was the pressure to be at the top of your game, all of the time, in order to not let down your peers.

The Secret Service culture, imbued into agents through the security advance model, is one of the primary reasons, in my opinion, that Secret Service agents overcome unimaginable threats to keep the President safe. It is also why many of the agents who have retired or resigned from the agency to take positions within the private sector have excelled in those positions. When you are a team member on a security advance for a high-threat-level Secret Service protectee, whether it be the President of the United States or the President of Iran, the attitude, on every team I have been part of is: "Not on our watch." In other words, no matter how much work it takes, the man or woman we are protecting is not going to be harmed "on our watch." It's not simply an agent culture sensitive to the fear of failure, in the eyes of your fellow agents, that motivates the agents. The results of every Secret Service agent's security advance are visible for everyone to see and, if the plan is an exceptional one, the other agents inevitably talk about it in glowing terms. Public praise does wonders for personal action when you are on the receiving end of it.

Depending on the threat level of a world leader the Secret Service is assigned to protect, the security advance team is generally broken down into specific, definable tasks, which all have an "advance team leader." All of these advance team members and the individual advance team leaders, whether they are responsible for motorcade security, physical security, communications security, hazardous agent mitigation or counter-sniper mitigation, all report to a lead advance agent and the pressure on him or her to succeed in the mission is transmitted throughout the team. The responsibility for these individual areas were the sole responsibility of the security advance team member charged with that specific portion of the security advance, regardless of the number of police officers, White House staffers, or military personnel he or she had working on that task. The proverbial "buck" stopped with them. There is no quicker way to ensure excellence in the performance of a task than to have the entire responsibility for its potential failure, and the full reward for its success, concentrated on one person. Reputation management is a full-time job in the Secret Service.

When I was conducting the physical security advance for President George W. Bush's visit to the Colombian Presidential Palace, the Casa de Nariño, during his visit with former Colombian President Álvaro Uribe Vélez, I was responsible for hundreds of military personnel, both U.S. and Colombian Secret Service agents, Colombian police and intelligence personnel, and White House and Colombian presidential staff members, but I knew if anything went wrong at the palace that the lead advance was coming right for me. Although this seems like a simple principle of leadership, in my experience in the private sector and in politics, I have seen a tendency to utilize team and matrix-type project models where the "team" is responsible for the successful completion of the task, but there is no further distillation of the task into specific, definable, and deliverable portions of the task, which team members can be held individually accountable for. There is nothing wrong with a team approach, the Secret Service's security advance team model is a team approach as well, but there is something very wrong with a team approach where the division of the labor is met by a misallocated division of the responsibility for the results of that labor. Divided labor is fine, but responsibility and accountability cannot be divided. Divided responsibility is no responsibility at all as no one person is fully accountable and, if the mission fails, there is an incentive to seek and partition blame. When a mission's success or failure is solely the responsibility of one person, then there is no one to partition the blame to; it's yours, you own it.

I have fond and distinct memories of that visit to Colombia by President George W. Bush to the Colombian Presidential Palace because it was the most difficult site security advance I conducted during my time in the Secret Service. Just five years earlier, on former Colombian President Uribe's inauguration day, in the same location at the Casa de Nariño, FARC (a Colombian terrorist group) guerillas fired mortar shells into the Casa de Nariño killing twenty-two and wounding sixty others. During the site security advance, I spent endless nights with little sleep, walking through in my mind, every detail of the palace. No corner, crevice, or closet escaped this mental exercise as I walked through every detail over and over again. During the day, while working on the plan within the palace I would think to myself, "What would I do right now if there were a terrorist assault team firing at us from that location?" I would ask myself other questions such as, "Where's the closest water source for decontamination" if the President was hit with a suspicious powder and, "Where's the thickest wall for a cover position if we had to move the President out of the line of fire?" At night I would rehearse this in my head in a manner probably no different than a ballet dancer rehearses every detail of her routine. This mental exercise was a key component of my preparation, as it was with many of my fellow agents, because we all knew that in the tragic event that the bullets started flying that there was going to be little time to think about what to do—there was only going to be time to react and that physical reaction is like flowing water, it will find the path of least resistance. The only way to decrease the "resistance" to effective action under severe stress is to have rehearsed the reactionary response so many times that it bypasses the resistance of conscious thought.

This endless planning and rehearsal was motivated by both a desire to show the agents I worked with on the Presidential Protective Division (PPD) that I could design an airtight security plan, and also by the dread of having to face Nate, the lead advance agent on the Colombia trip with a stellar reputation, and not having an answer to one of his questions. Nate was the agent who introduced me to the concept of "the big six." It was on that Colombia trip that he explained to me the need for a detailed plan to handle threats originating from "the big six"—tactical assaults, medical emergencies, chemical and biological threats, improvised explosive devices, airborne threats, and fire and geological threats. I had heard a number of agents break down their specific methods for security planning into various categories but Nate's "big six" always stuck with me and I use it to this day as a quick reminder when needed. I knew if I failed to answer one of Nate's detailed questions about a "big six" threat at the Colombian Presidential Palace that he would have given me a subtle look of disapproval. In the Secret Service, where your reputation is everything, that was all the motivation I needed to avoid any possibility of letting him down. We just didn't do that in the Secret Service and the difference between a great agent, a good agent, and a failure, was that the great agents never allowed this, the good ones rarely, and the failures simply didn't care either way and were quickly moved to positions where they could do the least damage. Notice, that for all of the time corporations and organizations spend on fancy compensation schemes through bonuses, stock options, and compensatory time off, it was largely the culture of excellence in the Secret Service through peer pressure and the public display of your work that motivated me and many others to do the job well. I am a steadfast believer in the power of the free market and the strong incentives it creates, but the soft skills of responsibility, personal accountability, and strong, forceful leadership cannot be developed using only financial rewards.

As I walked through the Casa de Nariño with President Bush behind me on March 11, 2007, and we traveled from room to room and meeting to meeting, and the plan unfolded seamlessly, I felt a sense of internal pride at what was accomplished. Watching my fellow PPD agents have a comfortable look on their faces within the giant entourage accompanying President Bush's every move, and knowing that no security "surprises" were going to appear was as satisfying a feeling as I've ever had as an agent. The agents had traveled most of the day and they were all tired. I could see the drawn looks on many of their faces as they stood for hours and never let their attention down for a moment. I asked many of the working PPD agents on that day if they wanted a "push" (Secret Service slang for a break) and, despite their obvious fatigue, not one of them accepted the offer. Not one of those agents was going to be the first one to sit down while the others remained on post. As President Bush was speaking at a press conference within one of the rooms, I noticed one of the agents at the corner of the room begin to sway a bit while standing still. The agents always tried to avoid swaying as to not distract the President when he was speaking, but when it did happen, it was a sure sign that the agent was tired and in pain. Swaying back and forth temporarily takes the pressure off your back and feet and provided a brief respite from the mismatch of leather-soled shoes and hard, marble floors. Having that same physically exhausted agent I watched swaying get back into the Secret Service follow-up vehicle hours later when President Bush left the palace and hearing the agent say, "Nice job," gave me a deeper satisfaction than any promotion or cash award could. In a culture where excellence is expected and failure is never an option, having another agent who subscribes to that same ethos, give you a sign of his approval is a reward I wouldn't have traded for anything at that moment. The Secret Service "culture" of success perpetuates, and continues to transmit through the organization, as you give those small signs of approval to other agents when you are the working shift at their security site. Individual success in an organization should never be kept a secret. I would rather work in an agency full of people anxiously seeking out public recognition for the hard work they do instead of working at an agency that worships mediocrity and encourages everyone to "not stand out." A logical response to the Secret Service model, which some looking to replicate may question, is: "If the advance team leader gets all the praise for a job well done, then what is the motivation for those working under him or her to do their jobs?" That's a fair question, but in my experience as an agent on those security advance teams, nearly everyone in a subordinate role witnessed personally, or heard secondhand, the compliments paid to the advance team leader as a result of their work and they all wanted to be a part of that experience when it was their turn. In order to make it to "the big show" (as the PPD agents jokingly called the division) and to be a part of the team, many of the agents knew that doing quality work in a subordinate role was the only path to that final destination and the only currency used to pay for the trip was their reputation.

Another component of the Secret Service security advance model, which instilled a culture of excellence in their agents, was their tendency to force leadership on their agents, and allow them to sink or swim, early in their careers. The Secret Service is not large enough (with just a little more than three thousand special agents) to allow agents to avoid responsibility completely. It is not uncommon for new agents, during an extremely busy protection period such as the United Nations General Assembly in New York City, to be assigned to a security advance team and be "thrown in the deep end of the pool" as one of the agents I worked with would often say. A seasoned Secret Service agent can tell in just a few hours who the successful protection agents are going to be and which agents are not going to cut it. This trial-by-fire process, whether by design or as a result of manpower necessities, is extremely efficient in separating the wheat from the chaff within the Secret Service. Word spreads quickly throughout the Secret Service if an agent shows promise early in their career because many of the divisions within the Secret Service are always looking to recruit the best new talent into their respective divisions. This early recognition of talent helps the service in allocating limited career development time and money to their best and brightest. As with many other public and private employers, the process of assigning agents to prestigious assignments within the agency is not free from a small degree of politics, nepotism, and favoritism, but I rarely saw an agent who was an above-average performer who was left out of a prestigious assignment. Within the Secret Service there was a parallel, informal process of career development that became known as "checking the box" that assisted the agents in knowing where they stood among their peers and served as a quasi "merit-badge" system. If a new agent was talented and willing to put in the work, he or she may be given a site security advance, then a motorcade advance, then a low-threat-level lead advance followed by a medium-threat-level lead advance, then, finally, a high-threat-level lead advance. Although none of these tasks involved a formal promotion it was not uncommon for an agent to ask one another, "Have you done a lead yet?" If you had done a high-threat-level lead advance and you were new to the Secret Service then that was a signal to everyone who knew about it that you were a top-tier performer. It was similar to walking around with a series of medals on your chest with no actual medals present, but everyone seeing them (the Secret Service e-mail system would announce these assignments and display your "medals" for you). Only in an environment where you are permitted to sink or swim early can the public recognition, and the positive work-culture externalities generated from that recognition, effectively change an organization.

It's unfortunate that many Americans view the government work as the home of mediocrity. While that may be the case in many departments and agencies, it was certainly not the case in the

Secret Service. Reform is possible and the lessons from the Secret Service security advance model are transportable. The Secret Service didn't invent personal accountability, division of labor, or trial-by-fire on-the-job training, but they slowly developed it within their workplace culture over time and created an environment where immersion in excellence and excuse avoidance, created a behavioral norm worth replicating.

3

The IRS Scandal—Have We Reached a Turning Point?

There are few things hardworking Americans fear more than an unexpected visit from the tax collector. The three words, Internal Revenue Service, can strike fear into the hearts of even the most emotionally hardened American citizens. Threats of confiscated earnings, jail time, endless litigation, and harassment all course through our minds when the IRS takes an interest in us. The power to take away your freedom, and your money, are awesome powers delegated to the IRS with the expected promise that this power will be respected and not irresponsibly abused. During my time with the Secret Service, I worked with a number of IRS special agents on joint financial crimes investigations and found them to be professional and well-versed in their responsibilities. Measuring by those positive experiences with the IRS agents I worked with, I was perplexed as to how the IRS targeting scandal (where director of the IRS Exempt Organizations Unit Lois Lerner apologized for the targeting of Conservative groups, stating it was "absolutely inappropriate") could have occurred. When I was a federal agent investigating a financial crimes case it was very difficult, and time consuming, to obtain the tax records of the people I was investigating, even when my case was airtight. To save time and move my investigations along at a productive pace, I typically ignored tax records in my investigations and used other means to solve a case due to the many requirements necessary to obtain tax records. If this was the case when I was a federal agent investigating very serious crimes, then how did the IRS manage to violate their creed and use confidential tax information to politically target President Barack Obama's political opponents? An experience I had during my special agent training may shed some light on this question.

Toward the end of my nine-month Secret Service special agent recruit-training program, my recruit class was taken on a tour of the new Secret Service headquarters building in Northwest Washington, DC. Ditching our khaki pants and white, polo-style Secret Service training shirts for our business suits, we all proudly strode through the lobby of the shiny, new headquarters building knowing that we were just weeks away from completing the training program and raising our right hands to swear in and formally join this elite law enforcement agency as new special agents. The beautiful new multistory headquarters building was an impressive structure and many of my classmates, who shared my very humble beginnings, were visibly proud to be in the building as employees and not tourists. The tour began in the Secret Service forensics laboratory where one of the technicians explained to us how to lift a fingerprint off of a document using their latest technology. The tour then worked its way through the director's office for a short pep talk, and we ended up in the protective intelligence section where the agent on duty explained to us how they investigated threats to the President. Having been both an undergraduate and graduate student in psychology, I found the content of the briefing fascinating and I was captivated by every word. In addition to the interesting content, up to this point in our training we had only heard about how threat investigations were done from the instructors in the classroom, not the agents actually doing them, and I wanted to see if the instructors were exaggerating when they told classroom "war stories."

The techniques the Secret Service uses in determining who is a legitimate threat to the President, and who is not, are the product of countless hours of both real-world threat investigation experience and detailed research on past assassination attempts both in the United States and in other countries. Their results are impressive considering the volume of threats they receive, the limited manpower resources they have, and that none of their special agents are professional psychologists. The briefing took a little while and I could tell that a number of the recruits were getting tired. We had been standing in leather-soled shoes, not designed for comfort, for most of the day and when the agent conducting the briefing took us into a conference room to sit down for the final portion of the briefing, we were all relieved. It was in this room when I realized how few internal controls exist to limit the growing power of the federal government and just how dangerous unchecked power can be.

The agent giving us the briefing began the final portion of the protective intelligence briefing with a detailed explanation of the investigative steps required to investigate a presidential threat case. He went through the importance of a potential assassin's travel history, the importance of their psychological history, and the grave importance of any potential assassin's familiarity with weapons. When he began to tell a story from a presidential threat case he had worked, he left us all with a "What would you do?" moment that changed everything for me. The intelligence agent explained how he had been engaged in a lengthy surveillance operation on a potentially serious presidential threat case and how the subject of the case had led him to a house. The subject was a threat, based on a number of factors, which can be red flags in presidential threat cases (i.e., a travel history mimicking the President's and the stalking of multiple targets), and the agent's concern was evident even in his recount of the long-since-passed events. When the subject arrived at the house the agent followed him and waited for him to come back out. As the time passed, and it was clear that the subject was not going to exit the home, the agent carefully approached the side of the home and looked in one of the windows. He told us that he saw a computer and what he could vaguely make out to be a work-in-progress letter on the computer screen. He explained that, based on his experience with the subject, he thought this was another threat letter to be sent to the President and asked us all, "What would you have done?" Nearly everyone raised their hands and had the correct answer; using the evidence you have accumulated, in conjunction with the new evidence, you get a search warrant. The agent agreed, but then said, "What if there's no time?" implying that there was an imminent threat to the life of the President. He then left us and asked us to think about it before our next class. It was an interesting question, which sparked a good amount of conversation among my classmates, but it was a remark made after the briefing concluded, that made me rethink the awesome power of a badge with a government seal on it. I'm absolutely sure the agent giving the briefing was joking, but someone asked him, as we were all leaving, what he would have done if this was happening right now and he said, laughingly, "Break the window and get the computer." No one took the comment seriously, or so I thought.

On the ride back later in the day with my fellow recruits, in the ugly, but spacious, dark-green passenger vans we used to travel around town, a fellow recruit asked me if I thought the instructor was serious about the "break the window" comment. I replied, "Of course not." That question changed how I perceived the power of the massive government bureaucracy I was about to join. I wondered, after that interaction, how many other offhand comments by people in positions of power and influence (instructors, supervisors, political appointees, and our President) within our federal government had been viewed as an imprimatur to violate the constitutional oath we all swore to uphold. Surely, the recruit in the van with me was not the only one who had made this mistake.

As the IRS targeting scandal of Conservative groups unfolded in 2013, I began to think about that intelligence briefing in Secret Service headquarters and how the majesty of the new shiny building, with the bold, protruding Secret Service star hanging on the wall in the lobby, and the halo of power surrounding the well-dressed and knowledgeable agent who made the offhand remark about "breaking the window," had all contributed to the recruit's misunderstanding of what he was entitled to do as a Secret Service agent. The recruit who thought that the "break the window" comment was serious was very intelligent and, from my experiences with him, he was a decent man with solid morals, yet he had fallen prey to the "just following orders" syndrome and he hadn't even begun his career as an agent yet. This willingness to consider, and accept, the power bestowed upon you, either legitimately or illegitimately, as a function of your service as an agent of the government is what our founding fathers feared. We are all fallible by nature and the corrupting influence of power is an inescapable part of our nature, as famously stated by Lord Acton in 1887: "Power tends to corrupt, and absolute power corrupts absolutely. Great men are almost always bad men." It is for this reason that the founders and crafters of our Constitution designed a system of separated powers where the accumulation of power by the federal government would be balanced against the interests and powers of the states, and the accumulation of power within any branch of our federal government could be checked and balanced by the power of the other branches. The IRS targeting scandal was a catastrophic breach of that delicate balance of power.

As the information on the IRS scandal involving the targeting of Conservative groups slowly leaked out I wondered if the scandal originated in the same way the intelligence briefing I attended as a Secret Service recruit did. Is it possible that, drunk with access to the President and his staff, and given access to roam the powerful halls of the White House, that an IRS manager had interpreted remarks relayed to him by a White House insider as an invitation to target the President's enemies? Did this manager think that the President would cover for him? I can imagine a scenario where a White House insider pulled the IRS manager aside and said, "Wouldn't it be ideal if we could just shut these Conservative groups down?" and the IRS manager, eager to impress, took it as an invitation to do just that. Do not underestimate the appeal within the federal government of feeling as if you are an integral part of "the team" when the magnetic attraction of proximity to power is involved. Even being seen with the President in a photo is a hot commodity in the halls of power in Washington, DC, and commodities such as this have a value, which can be traded for "favors."

Although I was sure at the time that the agent giving my recruit class the intelligence briefing was joking about the "break the window" comment, I frequently think, when considering the IRS case, "What if he wasn't joking about breaking the window?" What would I do if it were a real threat case against the President of the United States? Could the aura of power that had enveloped the agent, combined with the information asymmetry between me and him, where I believed he "knew what he was doing," lead me to believe that breaking the window was the right option because I was "just following orders"? Our federal government has grown so large and unaccountable that cases such as this are not beyond the realm of comprehension, and it is precisely because of these concerns that a limited federal government, with a well-defined and enforced system of checks and balances is a necessity, not an aspirational principle.

The IRS targeting scandal did not happen in a vacuum. The scandal happened under an administration where the sheer number of government scandals and abuses of power overwhelmed the institutional defense mechanisms designed to prevent this type of behavior. The massive failings of Obamacare, the Veterans Health Administration waiting lists, the Fast and Furious scandal, the GSA spending scandal, and the Benghazi attacks had both the U.S. Congress, and the American citizens, drinking from the proverbial "fire hose" as it relates to their ability to handle abuses of power. This is the critical paradox of big government Liberalism; the larger the government grows, the more abusive it becomes, and the less accountable and manageable it becomes as well. Public alarm bells should be loudly ringing as a result, but in speaking with self-declared Liberal members of the general public during my political campaigns, I was left with the impression by many of them that they believe there is some grand overseer policing potential abuses of power within the government. Although we have an Office of Inspector General within a number of Cabinet departments and government agencies, designed to weed out waste and mismanagement, we have congressional oversight, and we have an FBI, which investigates public corruption, the federal government has grown so vast and unaccountable that proper oversight is nothing but an impossible dream. The phenomena of regulatory capture (where government regulators are influenced by the people they are regulating due to their close working relationships and, importantly, the potential for a lucrative post-government career with the businesses they are regulating), the growing alphabet soup of federal agencies with their numerous, and sometimes overlapping assignments, the ability to remain relatively anonymous within the federal government as long as you limit your interactions with other federal personnel, and growing control emanating from Washington, DC, rather than locally, have all contributed to a severe lack of controls on federal government power. There are no angels ensuring that the original limited role of the federal government, which our founders envisioned, is strictly maintained. Fidelity to that vision is the responsibility of the citizen as well as the branches of government empowered by that vision. We have a Constitution, but sadly, it is being treated as a suggestion rather than a governing document to live by. Even our court system is limited in our current system. Our courts can strike down a law, or restrict the activities of our President based on a legal ruling, but the government bureaucracy has become so big and expansive that the avenues to overcome these temporary setbacks are numerous and inviting for the power hungry. We saw this with the Citizens United Supreme Court decision, which overturned some restrictions on independent political expenditures by corporations. Many believe that this setback to the Democrats in power, who despised this ruling, may have been the spark that lit the tinder, which set aflame the constitutionally protected liberties of the Conservative groups victimized in the IRS targeting scandal. If this was the case, as many believe, then the protections of our system of government are not only useless, but they are simply obstacles to be overcome in the quest for power by the Washington, DC, insider class.

4

Hitting the Emergency Brake on Out-of-Control Government

With the internal controls on the federal government's power failing, are there any external controls left? Voting is an external control, but voting without a properly informed electorate has become a poor mechanism for limiting the growing role of government in our lives. President Obama's political messaging team masterfully manipulated a relatively compliant mainstream media and succeeded in getting reelected despite a struggling economy, a bevy of scandals, a failing and eponymous healthcare reform plan, and a growing army of detractors. One of the few emergency brakes a free society has on government abuses is an activist media operation, which seeks out and reports the objective truth. An activist media, bent on exposing the many examples of government overreach and abuse could help turn this ship around and devolve some of the federal government's enormous power back to the states and the citizens.

There are few tools more powerful for restraining the behavior of those in power than the punishment, in the form of a dramatic change in public status, that a lawmaker experiences from the public humiliation when caught in a public corruption scandal. Unfortunately, many in the media have chosen to look the other way and chose to do the easy thing, and not the right thing when given the opportunity regarding the Benghazi terror attacks, the IRS scandal, the executive overreach with regard to President Obama's unilateral actions on Obamacare and immigration, and a host of other controversies where the President was given either a free pass or light coverage. Ironically, it is this same media that seems encouraged to do its job when there is a Republican in the White House and this may be our only saving grace as even politically skewed coverage of government abuse is better than no coverage at all. If you compare the media coverage of the Bush administration's allegedly politically motivated termination of a number of U.S. attorneys (a not-so-uncommon practice historically), with the coverage of the explosive IRS targeting scandal, you would think they were equally as detrimental to a properly functioning government. That is until you realize that U.S. attorneys serve as political appointees and can be dismissed by the executive branch for causes as the sitting President sees fit. You may not agree with those causes, and those causes may be unusual, but their dismissal is not a violation of the law. Yet, this story received a tremendous amount of media attention while the IRS targeting scandal was lightly covered by mainstream media outlets. If it weren't for the election of the occasional Republican president, I worry that the dangerous expansion of our federal government would be almost wholly unchecked by the external media control, which we expect, but have yet to fairly receive.

Having roamed the halls of power as a Secret Service agent, but never having been elected to use that power due to electoral losses, I worry about our future. While President Obama is neither the

first, nor the last president to attempt to expand the power of the
presidency at the expense of the legislative and judicial branches,
and the American people, I am concerned that we have reached
the point of no return. During my tenure as a former member of
the Presidential Protective Division, during a *Marine One* landing
on the White House South Lawn, one of the local Washington, DC,
"assets" we used during the landings was late to the assignment. I
struck up a conversation with a local Washington, DC, Metro police
officer about the asset being late and we were both disappointed
that it had failed to arrive on time. I told him that we needed to
treat every single presidential visit as if it were the first presidential visit on the day after someone tried to assassinate the President.
This was a saying that I had heard many times from experienced
agents regarding the security of presidential motorcades while assigned to the transportation section of the PPD, and it served as a
pointed reminder of the gravity of our mission. This saying was
meant to convey the larger idea that we are living with a crisis-
driven government that can't manage even its most basic tasks any-
more and can only react to a crisis, in this case a potential attack
on the President. Many of the rank-and-file Secret Service agents
could pinpoint holes in the White House security plan, but felt that
speaking out would label them "complainers" and the aforementioned saying implied that nothing would change until, heaven
forbid, some attack happened. We all witnessed this dynamic play
out with the White House fence-jumping incident on the North
Grounds. This concerns me, and should concern you, because this
crisis-driven government we are forced to live with frequently
fails to do its job, and when it's caught not doing its job, it over-
reacts by leveraging the crisis as a medium to attack our liberty
and freedom. Making matters worse is the tendency for government

insiders to act as the Secret Service recruit, who had mistaken the "break the window" comment from the intelligence agent as an actual guideline, and to assume the potentially unlawful orders they have been given pursuant to a crisis have been vetted through the massive government bureaucracy and are legitimate. Why question the constitutionality of an order when it appears to have worked its way through the labyrinthine government bureaucracy and passed through multiple channels? If it made it to your desk, as the government employee charged with carrying out the order, then of course it must be a legitimate order. Sounds reasonable.

When I read through the publicly available information on the genesis of the IRS targeting scandal and the privacy abuses at the National Security Agency, I am saddened at what the future may hold if there is not a renewed media interest in bipartisan investigative journalism and genuine congressional oversight. If there is one thing nearly every lawmaker and political staff member in Washington, DC, fears, it's being on the front page of a newspaper for wrongdoing.

It's breathtaking how often our government is caught red-handed lying to us. Whether it's the infamous President Obama "If you like your plan, you can keep your plan" Obamacare promise, or the assurances from the NSA director that the NSA has been "fully compliant with the law," despite evidence of obvious violations, Americans are rapidly losing faith in their government. Once that faith is lost it is difficult to regain. Sometimes, we take for granted the integrity of our institutions in the United States as if it's the rule and not the global exception it is. Thankfully, cases of public corruption involving elected officials, judges, and law enforcement are still relatively rare occurrences in the United States. But the damage that the Obama administration has done to the public's trust in the integrity and fairness of our federal government institutions is grave and will take time to repair. Once we, as a society, lose faith in government, the economic dislocations and political gamesmanship start to spiral out of control. It quickly becomes far more profitable to invest in political connections than to invest in your business or employees. Entire industries develop around learning to leverage political connections to expedite the machinery of government when the bureaucracy drives nearly everything to a slow grind. Political recrimination becomes commonplace and fear becomes a natural response when any agent of the government intentionally crosses your path in a broken system like this.

Traveling as a Secret Service agent, I visited a number of countries where their institutions were rife with corruption and I remember being disturbed by the willingness of the citizenry to accept it as the price of "doing business." During an extended stay in Russia with an agent named "Steve," we came into direct contact with a system such as this. Steve and I were on a temporary investigative assignment in Russia, which was scheduled to last for three weeks, and during our first few days in the country, we were reluctant to travel around in the Secret Service embassy car alone because we were unfamiliar with the streets. Compounding the difficulty was the fact that neither Steve nor I spoke any Russian. The office manager, Elena, who had lived in Russia as an ex-pat with her husband and daughter, was helpful in assisting Steve and me in getting around the streets of Moscow and we frequently took her with us. It was obvious to Steve and me that we were followed most of the time, most likely by the Russian FSB (the former KGB), but they were not aggressive with us and as time passed we saw them less as a nuisance and more as an asset. After approximately three weeks in Russia, Steve and I began to get adventurous and started to travel around, although we were still uncertain where we were going. To be honest, we probably went out because we were bored from being stuck in hotel rooms during long weekends.

Driving around Moscow, it was impossible to miss the police officers, and their ubiquitous white sticks. These sticks they carried seemed to have a near magical power over the residents of Moscow because if a police officer waved or pointed his white stick at a driver or pedestrian, they instantly stopped. Steve and I initially chuckled when we saw it until we began to realize that its "magical power" was likely the result of a police department with few controls on what that stick would do to a Moscow resident if they didn't stop immediately. It became even less humorous when, after driving around Moscow after an assignment, Steve and I had the white stick waved at us. While driving, we got lost and we made an illegal U-turn trying to get back to the hotel and didn't notice the police officer in his car right in front of where we turned. We watched him get out of his car with the white stick and wave at us to pull over. We pulled over on a small bridge over water and, as he approached, we were both mildly concerned but not yet overly anxious. The Russian police officer was a portly man, poorly outfitted with his two-sizes-too-big uniform and a rough demeanor to match. As Steve slowly rolled down the window the Russian police officer began to aggressively gesture to us and loudly yell at us in Russian. We assumed he was cursing at us because we couldn't understand a word he was saying, but he was saying it loudly and forcefully while making frantic gestures. As the minutes passed, and the yelling continued, Steve and I began to talk about what we should do realizing that the officer spoke no English. The

Russian police officer didn't respond to what we were saying so we continued speaking to each other in English as if he weren't there. This appeared to infuriate him even more as his tone got louder and louder and his gestures more animated. Steve and I had diplomatic passports, giving us some degree of diplomatic immunity, but we were concerned that the police officer didn't give a hoot about our diplomatic status as he began to gesture toward our pockets. Steve and I both interpreted this as the universal symbol for "Give me some of your money and I'll go away," and based on his response when we pointed to our pockets, we were correct. He was clearly looking for a bribe, which neither Steve nor I was going to pay. We kept pointing to our pockets telling him, "No," but that only made him angrier as he realized that his easy payday was not forthcoming. It was at this point where Steve and I began to seriously consider how we were going to get out of this. We had been there for about twenty-five minutes and the police officer was not budging in his demand for a quick payoff. We anxiously joked, "Maybe we should throw him in the water and take off," but that silly caper quickly went nowhere as we pondered the ramifications of spending the rest of our lives in a Siberian prison. At this point, Steve decided to call the U.S. Marine Corps stationed at the U.S. Embassy "Post One" in Moscow (this is who you're trained to call at the Embassy if things break bad overseas) and the act of making the phone call must have worried the bribe-seeking police officer. The officer walked back to his car, talking to himself in a frustrated manner, and just minutes later he returned and threw a traffic ticket in our faces, disappointed he was not leaving with a fatter wallet. Unfortunately, this is daily life in corrupt countries where the rule of law is discretionary and government institutions are failing their people. Steve and I were on an official U.S.

government assignment, and holding diplomatic passports, and the police officer cared only about the bribe as if codes of conduct and international order didn't even exist. The people walking on the bridge near us when we were pulled over saw nothing unusual with what was going on, either, as they simply went about their business. Although I have faith that our police officers in the United States are cut from a different cloth due to their education and training, I wonder how long we can all be expected to blindly follow the law when the people elected to write the laws and enforce them ignore them. Disrespect for law and order starts at the top and sets the stage for a general climate of fear and distrust. Using the tools of government to target innocent Americans, and suffering virtually no tangible consequences for it, is but one of the ways that the virus of government mistrust began with patient zero in the White House.

Many of us, having never lived under an alternative system where the media is not free to operate absent government pressure, have not properly processed the dangers in continuing down this path. When I would travel on *Air Force One* as a Secret Service agent, we would be seated in an adjoining area to where the White House traveling press corps were seated and, in listening to some of their conversations, it became clear how a media theme could spread like a virus throughout their coverage of an event. The White House traveling press corps live, work, and travel together, read each other's coverage of an event, and, if the majority of the traveling press are covering an event with an optimistic and upbeat tone, there appeared to be a tacit peer pressure working to cover it in the same way. The problem is magnified when the theme is chosen not by the press, but by self-interested political players. There is no emergency brake on government abusing its power if the handle on the emergency brake is being held by those in power, and not those in the press covering those in power.

I saw an example of this firsthand during a security advance team operation I was part of during my tenure on the PPD. On the visit, I was assigned to conduct the transportation advance and secure the motorcade route for the visit to a formerly communist country by President George W. Bush, near the end of his time in office. When we conduct these overseas security advances we work through the U.S. Embassy staff to acquire a "foreign counterpart" for each component of the advance team to assist us in navigating around the foreign legal, military, and law enforcement infrastructure. Each component of the Secret Service advance team presents unique complications on foreign soil. The counter-sniper teams may need access to rooftops in a country where the building owner can refuse to comply. Given the fact that the Secret Service has no law enforcement authority in these foreign countries, we heavily rely on our foreign security or military counterparts to "grease the skids" when needed. The term "grease the skids" took on a new meaning during this visit and served as a reminder to me of the importance of a vibrant free press.

While conducting a Secret Service motorcade advance, it is beneficial to select a travel route as early in the advance as possible because the drivers and the advance agents must drive the motorcade route countless times to familiarize themselves with every terrain feature along the route, and methodically allocate assets along the route according to security needs. The Secret Service drivers must know the streets in a foreign country with the same level of familiarity as if they grew up on them. Some portions of the route will use more manpower and equipment assets because of the ability of a potential assassin to hide along the route (i.e., forests, densely populated streets) or because of the necessity of the motorcade to slow down (i.e., sharp turns in the roads). However, selecting the President's route of travel early in the security advance creates a number of information security problems for the transportation advance agent. The advance agent must avoid allowing the information to prematurely leak out because this gives any potential assassin time to plan for any potential attack on the motorcade, and any movements by the advance agents along the chosen route can telegraph where the President is going to be. To remedy this, we pick a number of routes and alternate routes and do our best to avoid telegraphing which one we will choose.

This operation presented a number of additional security complications because we were extremely limited in the number of available motorcade route options, and they were all less than ideal. The thin streets and the proximity of the potential crowds to President Bush's limousine increased the danger level of the operation and, as a result, I used extraordinary efforts to keep the exact route we planned to use a secret. My plans were thrown into disarray when, just days before the President was scheduled to land, news of the President's intended motorcade route began to leak out. I was running out of time and changing the entire route was not an option at this point in lieu of a substantial security reason and, as a result, I aired my concerns to my foreign law enforcement counterpart. He had been a law enforcement operator under the formerly communist government and, in my dealings with him, I understood him to be a serious man, but a man with a far different idea of what a free press was. He told me not to worry about it, that he had "contacts" in the media and that he would help. I wasn't exactly sure what "help" meant, but out of necessity, I was willing to let him try. When I awoke the next day, I was surprised to see a map of President Bush's motorcade route published in one of the local papers and thought to myself, "This is help?" But upon closer inspection of the map in the newspaper, I noticed that it wasn't our motorcade route. I had no idea what motorcade route this newspaper thought they were printing, but it most certainly was not ours. At a lunch with my foreign counterpart later in the day it became obvious what had happened. Although the country had abandoned communism, the remnants of its pernicious state/media symbiosis were still lurking and it appeared that some in the country's media operation were still taking phone calls from the law enforcement arm of the state, and eager to do its bidding. My counterpart was quiet about the details of his subterfuge operation therefore I'll never be certain as to how that faux motorcade route made it into the newspaper, but even though the incident helped me get the President in and out of the country safely, I was always troubled by it and it always reminded me of the importance of keeping the press free from the influence of government, even when trying to "help."

This expansion of federal power, with the tacit compliance of our media, will eventually come to haunt the media figures who have treated both the Democratic Party and President Obama as fragile pieces of china. As we saw with the Associated Press phone records scandal during the Obama administration, it is only a matter of time before the person the media attempts to shield, throws that shield back at them. Once the erosion of liberty begins, it is nearly impossible to stop the process without an outcry from the public. That public cannot scream for help if the media insists on hiding the information from those who need it, and muffling the screams of those who have it. As I learned from that recruit in the training van on the way back from the Secret Service headquarters briefing, when someone from the government tells you to "break the window" you had better call someone you trust first, and make sure you're doing the right thing. The public used to trust the media and it will be a long time before that trust is reestablished if they continue down the path of feigned ignorance.

5

The White House Drone Crash and the Coming Privacy Nightmare

At approximately 3:00 a.m. on Monday, January 26, 2015, a two-foot-long, commercially available, quadcopter drone crashed onto the sprawling South Grounds of the White House complex after being spotted by a Secret Service Uniformed Division officer. Although the incident was downplayed by the White House, Pandora's box had been opened at the White House and the entire world saw what was inside. I woke at 5:30 a.m. on January 26, 2015, just hours after the drone crash at the White House and I found out about it as I was preparing to do a morning interview with CNN. The scheduled interview was about a police use-of-force incident involving a New York media figure's son, but I received a text from a CNN producer asking me about "the device at the White House." When I read the details of the incident, I knew that this was a game-changing moment for not only the Secret Service, but for law enforcement, military, and security professionals everywhere.

The Secret Service is staffed with highly qualified agents who spend the majority of their time thinking through potential attack and mitigation scenarios involving the many bizarre and creative ways potential assassins can inflict disaster upon their protectees. But drone technology creates a number of unique security headaches for the Secret Service. Many of these problems became apparent on the night of the drone crash. Any object that can transport, or hide, surveillance technology or weapons (everything from airplanes and cars to suitcases and unattended packages) will always be a concern for security professionals, but drones are especially concerning because of their size, obtainability, and detectability. Planes and automobiles can carry explosives toward a secure facility in the form of a car bomb or through a plane's fuel tank in a suicide mission, but they are both large enough to be detected or mitigated in advance if the proper security protocols are followed. It takes time to circumvent security precautions on a plane. Whether it's the air traffic control monitoring the flight path of the plane or the airport security mechanisms monitoring the passengers flying on the plane, these security precautions buy time and time is necessary to implement a successful attack. A warning from air traffic control or from the TSA creates time and this time, however brief, frequently avails the security operation of some warning and time to respond. Drones offer none of this because they are difficult to detect due to their size and they are easily acquired and operated. There is no airport TSA magnetometer to circumvent, no air traffic control operator to deceive, no pilot training required, and as quickly as the drone appears at the White House or some other secure location, its explosive payload can be detonated with little warning.

While explosive transporting drones present new airborne explosive threats, drone technology also presents surveillance threats. This technology is leading us down a road where insect-sized surveillance drones could land on your shoulder, without your knowledge, with little warning, and record every action and word you do and say. Whereas this technology offers tremendous tactical advantages to our military on the field of battle, and to law enforcement in their quest for a wider and more undetectable surveillance net, it also offers countless opportunities for intelligence and blackmail for those among us with malicious intent. How many of you would be comfortable if your every private moment was recorded?

Technology has always been a sword with a sharp double edge. It will inevitably bring us into a future where our food, energy, transportation, and entertainment needs and wants will be far less constricted than they are today. But technology, as we have seen with the rapidly evolving drone threat, is also leading us down the road to a future where security and privacy will have to be bought, and the market solutions will be in short supply and in high demand. Many of the physical and technical mechanisms we use today to build our secure environments at airports, government facilities, courts, sporting and entertainment events, and around our elected officials, will be obsolete in the very near future due to rapidly evolving technologies, which can easily circumvent these traditional firewalls. Compounding the problem is the explosive growth in information technology and rapid information transfer through the Internet. This has created a virtually open forum to share techniques for defeating and evading traditional physical and technological security mechanisms we have come to rely on. It has also become a breeding ground for the interception of, and trading in, both personal and corporate information obtained illicitly. The hacking of Sony, and the subsequent release of sensitive e-mails and corporate secrets, will become ubiquitous in the future and anyone with a public profile will become a potential target for

bribery and extortion through the hacking of their personal communications.

One of the ironies of the unfolding surveillance state (both
government surveillance and private surveillance) is that a blurry
distinction between the "public self" and the "private self" was
once the near-exclusive hallmark of totalitarian regimes and
command-and-control economies. We all have a "public self" and
that "public self" acts and speaks far differently than the "private
self" does. As citizens of the United States, a constitutional Republic, we understand the distinction between how we act when we
know, or feel, that we are being watched and when we are confident that we are alone. This confidence, that we are alone and
behaving as the private self, is not a feeling shared by people who
were reared under the heavy hand of government in totalitarian
regimes where friends, family, and neighbors are taught that their
most important loyalty is to the state. This perverted sense of
loyalty to the state over all encourages those friends, family, and
neighbors to report on any acts of perceived subversion or insub-
ordination. The psychological ramifications to a person's sense of
privacy and individuality are devastating from the many personal
accounts I have heard from people raised under oppressive state
regimes. The unparalleled success of our mix of relatively free
markets and representative democracy has created a country so
prosperous that the destruction of the private self in the United
States, through developments in surveillance technology, may result in the same devastating psychological fallout in the future,
even though the origins of that destruction come from the private
sector and not the state. What were considered to be exclusively
personal e-mail, voice, and text interactions in the past will be
handled with skepticism by both parties to the conversation as the

potential for uninvited monitoring by third parties becomes more likely. Business meetings will never be the same for companies that could potentially have the full contents of their meetings disclosed for the world to see as surveillance technology advances and miniaturizes. The surveillance future will also create new opportunities for Peeping Tom types who are no longer limited by the height of your windows and their eyes.

None of this is new to the thousands of federal agents and military and intelligence personnel who have traveled extensively as part of their job routine. As a Secret Service agent on foreign visits, I was always briefed by the State Department's Diplomatic Security Service, within hours of landing in a new country, about the threat of both physical and technical surveillance during my stay in the respective country. I recall a visit to a country in Asia where I was shown some very revealing pictures by an ARSO (Assistant Regional Security Officer) of the Diplomatic Security Service of an American businessman with an attractive woman who was not his significant other. The ARSO explained to me that the hotel room had been wired for video and sound and that the businessman was the unlucky target of an intricate corporate espionage and bribery attempt. But to set up a surveillance operation such as this, traditionally took some modicum of skill, effort, and technological savvy to wire the room for sound and video and to prepare it for the operation. The new, user-friendly, and increasingly unnoticeable camera and video technology being developed will render the costs of these types of operations minimal and the potential rewards, if they catch the right fish in their surveillance net, substantial. Corporate and government secrets will no longer be secret unless costly and time-consuming surveillance countermeasures are employed.

This surveillance future will spawn an industry of detection devices for security professionals, businesses, and for the general public alike. These detection devices will likely be built into wearable and portable devices and we will be living far different public lives in the future as we are made aware, by our own personal surveillance detection equipment, of the ongoing monitoring of our behavior by the growing network of cameras and sensors. No business meeting or personal interaction in the future can be expected to remain private as a cottage industry of cameras and recorders, and detection equipment meant to detect them, sprouts and grows. Sony, and former Los Angeles Clippers owner Donald Sterling, who was surreptitiously recorded in a racist rant with his former girlfriend, are harbingers of what's to come in a future where private conversations can become public scandals with the simple click of a mouse.

In addition to the problems presented by a sprawling surveillance environment, today's physical security infrastructure will be rendered useless in the future by technological developments in weapons construction. A significant portion of our physical security infrastructure has been built around the detection of metals by magnetometer sensors, and metals have almost always served as building materials for weapons both crude and advanced. The advent of three-dimensional printing devices in manufacturing using complex, nonmetallic polymers will render this metal-detection security infrastructure useless. It will also create another serious problem for security and law enforcement personnel: proliferation. Acquiring a personal firearm today, even in the locations with the most lenient firearm regulations, requires some degree of interaction either with a registered federal firearms dealer or with a private citizen currently in possession of the firearm during the purchase or exchange. Illegally trafficking in firearms also carries enormous risk because the firearms must be transported from point A to point B and movement creates the potential for unplanned interactions with the police and civilians, which could lead to arrest. The rapidly growing technology behind three-dimensional printing is going to render many of these movement and interaction risks moot in the very near future. Acquiring a firearm will be as simple as acquiring the three-dimensional printing hardware and the software code to print the firearm in the safety of your own home or office. And, while law-abiding owners of firearms will continue to be subjected to federal and state regulations on the acquisition of the software firearm codes, criminals and terrorists will print the firearms they need, on demand, with the printed firearms being virtually undetectable using current metal-detection technology. In this future, which I have described, every potential criminal or terrorist with access to the three-dimensional printing hardware and software has the potential to become an arms dealer as well. This future creates a conundrum for elected officials, law enforcement, militaries, and security personnel because, even if you could detect the presence of the three-dimensional printed firearm, using newer detection equipment, how do you handle the presence of a three-dimensional printer in a future where they are sure to be ubiquitous? Will the three-dimensional printer be regulated like firearms are regulated today? The answers here are not comfortable and I am not advocating for any specific regulation on three-dimensional printers, I am simply presenting options, which I am sure will be discussed by those desperate for a solution to a surveillance and weapons proliferation future that is rapidly approaching.

The evolution of sensors as a result of the slow technological divorce between metal firearms and explosives is already happening. We already have this technology at some airports where they have employed backscatter X-ray technology. Backscatter X-ray technology enables security officials to see the form of a weapon or bomb through a person's clothing, but how comfortable are you in a future where this technology is present at the entrance to every government building and business that can afford one? Sadly, I can envision a future where an illicit trade in the clothing-free backscatter X-ray images of everyday Americans becomes commonplace due to the need for new imaging technology. Combine this with the growing use of high-definition cameras by both public and private operators and a surveillance future where your life outside of your front door is recorded by detection equipment, sensors, and cameras, and you can see how the concept of "privacy," as we know it now, will only be a history lesson.

6

Istanbul, Bowe Bergdahl, and the Unforgivable Sin

When I was an instructor in the Secret Service training academy in Prince George's County, Maryland, I noticed a pattern among the new recruits. The recruits entering duty with the Secret Service from a prior assignment with the U.S. military, regardless of their age, were consistently better prepared for the rigors of Secret Service agent training than their fellow recruits from other professions. Whenever there was a leadership void in one of the many practical exercises we would do with the trainees, it was frequently a recruit who was a former member of the military who would jump in and take charge of the situation. Some would even take charge of a situation that they were not in charge of the moment they detected that the leader of the task was a weak link. It would be difficult to distill down to a few overly simplified bullet points why the military training regimen and work atmosphere embed leadership qualities in military personnel, but having observed many of them in action in stressful scenarios, it appeared to be influenced by a strong desire to avoid letting their teammates down. The Secret Service training program has done

its best to emulate this paramilitary training model and to ensure that these "team-first" qualities are core components of their
agent's job ethos. As I stated earlier in the book, divided labor
within a team is fine, but divided responsibility is a deal breaker,
and training agents to never let their fellow agents down on an
operation is a crucial component of this. When you are given a task
as an agent on a mission, then you own that task; it's yours. If the
ultimate responsibility for a task falls to "the team," and not an
individual, then the weakest members of the team have an excuse
to avoid actively participating in the task and working to ensure a
positive outcome. The importance of "the team" was consistently
reinforced throughout the Secret Service recruit-training program
and in their on-the-job training regimen, but the importance of the
team was always stressed as a collection of individual responsibilities and contributions toward a larger goal. The concept of "the
team" in the Secret Service training model is everywhere in the
training program, even the method by which the Secret Service
agent recruits are trained to surround and walk with the President;
when the President moves, it is a team exercise. Every protection
agent's pattern of walking in the formation around the President
is determined by how other team members in the formation respond to the President's movements. It is a delicate ballet with no
room for error. When mistakes are made, security holes appear and
the person creating the hole has let "the team" down and everyone
in the formation can see it.

Knowing that your individual responsibility for the proper completion of a task is pivotal toward effectively completing a mission, and that the success or failure of your task will be exclusively
your responsibility, is a powerful motivator to get the job done correctly in the Secret Service. I felt this pressure to perform through-

out my career as an agent but it was during one specific trip that this pressure to perform for the sake of the team resulted in long-term physical consequences.

In June 2004 President George W. Bush attended the NATO summit in Istanbul, Turkey, and I was selected as a security agent on the visit. The trip was a security nightmare from the announcement of the summit onward, but given the agents of the Secret Service's penchant for seeking out adventure, the visit to Istanbul became a coveted operation among agents clamoring to be a part of it. Foreign security advances, even in countries considered relatively friendly to the United States, in the Secret Service are the most difficult protection operations we conduct. They are so detailed that a "go-by" (Secret Service lingo for a "to-do" list) I had prepared to help guide me through the many complicated tasks involved in a foreign security advance had grown to approximately fifty pages in length when I left the Presidential Protective Division.

I was selected, along with a few of my coworkers from the Secret Service training center in Maryland (largely because of the Secret Service training academy's proximity to Joint Base Andrews, known at the time as Andrews Air Force Base), to go on the Istanbul trip because it was cheaper for the Secret Service to fly us to Istanbul from Joint Base Andrews in Maryland, than to fly agents from field offices around the country. Agents from the training academy were also valuable on dangerous foreign visits because we all had a few years of experience, which was a prerequisite for foreign trips with this type of threat profile.

The two agents from the training academy assigned to the Istanbul operation with me—Tim and Curtis—were good friends of mine, but they had very different paths to the Secret Service, both contrasting sharply with my path. Tim was a Midwesterner with a heavy dose of accent and a heavier dose of leadership ability. He was a U.S. Marine and former police officer and he had an uncanny ability to tell you the truth regardless of how you were going to feel when he was done telling you the truth. I've heard people state many times that they want the truth from their friends and associates, but I found the opposite to be true. People want to be flattered and lied to when the truth is uncomfortable, but Tim had no time for that. I admired his ability to forgo easy promotion through the ranks in the Secret Service in exchange for his determination to do, and say, the right thing when the right thing mattered. Any fool can do the right thing when the consequences are irrelevant, but Tim had no problem telling a well-connected White House staffer that he or she was wrong, even when he knew that the staff member would try to blackball him as "difficult." Curtis was a U.S. Marine as well and was raised in the South. They were both good friends and I enjoyed their company, but I knew there would be some hijinks during the trip because Tim loved to mess around with Curtis, in contrast to his otherwise solemn and serious personality. When we landed on the ground in Istanbul it didn't take long for Tim to lighten up the deadly serious environment on the ground, at Curtis's expense. When we hit the ground in Istanbul after a long flight on an old military C-5 cargo plane (where you ride in the upper section of the plane facing backward, which makes for an unusual flying experience the first time you do it) we were immediately met by the Secret Service lead intelligence agent on the ground for a briefing. It was always a dramatic sight standing in the belly of a C-5 after landing on a long flight and watching the nose of the plane separate and lift up. The sun and the air would rapidly rush into the plane as if you were in a sealed box and the top was removed and the agents on the ground would magically appear walking into the plane silhouetted by the sun in the background. Concerned about the visit, I had done some homework on the trip before leaving Joint Base Andrews, but I hadn't seen the classified information on just how dangerous this trip was going to be, and I was about to find out just how dangerous from the team on the ground. Approximately one year before the Istanbul visit, a series of truck bombs in the country had killed and injured hundreds, and just hours before we landed on the ground, a series of explosions in both Ankara (outside of the hotel President Bush was scheduled to stay at) and in Istanbul had caused mayhem and death. One month prior to the trip a terror cell was arrested and found in possession of firearms, explosives, and terror training materials, and only one day into the trip, a bomb was found at Istanbul's airport. But the icing on the cake was a comment from one of the agents on the trip, who had arrived in Istanbul a few weeks before us. I asked him if the hotel we were staying in was safe, and he said, "A few bombs went off recently outside of the hotel, but we're pretty sure they were just noisemakers."

"Noisemakers?" I thought. "Is he serious?" He was definitely serious. These "noisemakers" were explosives more intended to frighten than to cause damage and gauging by the lack of emotion in the agent telling me the story, the attempt to cause fear hadn't worked, at least on him.

With this backdrop of danger, and the potential for a deadly terror strike hanging over the trip, the agents who arrived on the C-5 were noticeably concerned. But it was considered extremely bad form in the Secret Service to show that you were intimidated by your surroundings, it was the equivalent of letting down "the team" by showing fear. Visibly showing fear was seen as unnecessarily panicking the security team and it was irrelevant to the completion of the mission, which had to be completed regardless of how concerning the threat atmosphere was. The Secret Service was going to make sure that President Bush arrived and departed Istanbul without a scratch and worrying about your own safety was seen as selfish and distracting. As a result, we all kept quiet about our concerns.

Tim, always the prankster with Curtis, decided that he would turn the screws on Curtis and co-opted me into a prank he planned. The prank was a welcome reprieve from the tension on the visit and I happily joined in. Tim and I were in a small shop in the lobby of the hotel we were staying in and I asked the female shopkeeper to see a small gem she had. The shopkeeper took me to the back of the store where Tim and I disappeared for a moment. Curtis saw us disappear for a moment because when we emerged he asked us where we had gone and looked concerned. Tim decided this was the time to strike. He told Curtis to hold on and took me to the side and said, "Brother, we gotta do this. Let's tell Curtis that the shopkeeper took us to the back of the store because she knew the hotel cameras were watching and cryptically warned us to '*Beware of the Ishirahe.*'" I asked him what the hell the "Ishirahe" was and he laughed with that hearty Midwestern belly laugh and said back, "I have no freakin' idea, I just made it up. Let's tell him we think it's some group following us around the hotel." It was terrible humor, and we both knew it, but we knew Curtis would eat it up. Tim told Curtis the story and I could see the look on Curtis's face, and it was priceless. Curtis was a tough guy and he wasn't going to show any fear, but we could tell it hit him hard. I know this attempt at humor, at Curtis's expense, may sound a bit strange to people who have never been in these types of situations, but many of the military, intelligence, and law enforcement men and women I've worked with have various ways of relieving stress and showing friendship toward their teammates that defy a rational explanation. Even though Curtis was concerned, both Tim and I refused to let the joke go too far before we blew the gag. We both liked Curtis and this was some strange ritual that we used as an expression of camaraderie and friendship, although I'm aware that it may seem counterintuitive. Tim and I let Curtis off the hook about twenty minutes later to which he replied, "You guys are morons."

The time for humor quickly came to an end a few days after our arrival in Istanbul when the mission was scheduled to start. In the Secret Service "wheels down" (a term we used for when *Air Force One* would arrive with the President onboard) was always on our minds in the planning process days before the visit and we would count down to "wheels down" with meetings and "walk-throughs." Walk-throughs were similar to full dress rehearsals of the security plan and during a walk-through at a soccer field where our helicopters were going to land I felt an extremely unusual and painful twinge in my spine. I had severe back problems as a result of an injury I sustained during my Secret Service recruit-training class's fitness test, when I attempted to achieve a score of "Excellent" in the sit-and-reach flexibility test and forced myself to push a small, flexibility measuring lever farther than my spine would allow. I had caused a severe bulge in two spinal disks as a result and my back was never the same. Back injuries are life-changing because there is no way to work around them. You can immobilize a bad arm or ankle, but your spine is what keeps it all together and when I had a "bad back day" it was torturous. The twinge

I felt kept getting worse throughout the walk-through and I prayed that I could get through the very dangerous Istanbul trip without being a burden to the operation or the team so I kept it quiet initially.

The following day we returned to the soccer field, awaiting the arrival of the President and the entourage, and after dealing with the massive amounts of dirt and dust thrown in my sweaty face from the rotor wash from the helicopters, I asked the agents coming off the "birds" (as we would call the helicopters) what I could do to help. He threw me one of the twenty-five-plus-pound first aid kits we would carry in the event of an emergency and asked me to carry it. We had a steep hill to walk up and it was a hot and humid day. The walk up the hill was only a couple of hundred yards, but with my back really bothering me, it felt like a lot longer. About fifty yards into the walk up the hill, I felt it. I knew it was different this time. I felt a powerful twinge in my spine like I hadn't felt before and I knew something had happened. It was game time, and now that President Bush had just landed and despite the pain, I kept on smiling although I was quietly in excruciating pain. I knew that no one walking up that hill with me to the awaiting vehicles wanted to be burdened with any concern for my back. These agents were from the Presidential Protective Division and had all of the same threat assessment briefings I did. They knew the danger level on the trip. The PPD agents were the best the Secret Service had to offer and they always acted as such. They walked with a noticeable swagger and they could be an intimidating group to talk to when you weren't a part of their team (something I tried to change later when I became a senior agent on the President's detail) and I wasn't going to be the one to break the icy look on their faces with a comment about my injured back. I stayed quiet during the ride to the hotel and I tried to avoid squirming in the car to avoid drawing attention to myself, although my back was begging me to move in order to relieve the unbearable pressure on my spine from sitting squished between two large male agents. The moments in the car seemed like hours and the pain in my back made me completely forget the dangers involved in the trip, which were now magnified because the world's number one target, the U.S. President, was on the ground. Arriving at the hotel, I slowly moved to my room to avoid causing a scene and aggravating what I knew was a serious injury, and while in the elevator I began to anxiously wonder how I was going to make it through this trip. I was now in severe pain and my assignments over the next few days involved hours of standing and being distracted by pain in such a dangerous environment was not an option. I closed the door to my room and took off my suit jacket and dress shirt revealing a thick, white level-3, bullet-resistant vest on top of a white T-shirt soaked in sweat from the heat. When I took off the vest and the underlying T-shirt, and the cold air from the room's air-conditioning hit my still moist skin, I dropped in pain. My back muscles on my left side of my lower back immediately seized up and tilted me sideways in a painful spasm. I thought that if I toughed it out for a few minutes that it would relent and I would be able to stand up, but as the minutes passed, I knew that standing was going to be impossible. Now I was stuck and I knew that I had done the unforgivable; I was going to become a liability on this trip, rather than an asset, and I was going to let down the team. Secret Service training does that to the agents. I should have been more concerned with my spine and the damage that I had done to it walking up that steep hill, with an injured back, and carrying an unbalanced load in one hand while walking in dress shoes, but I wasn't. I was in pain, but I was worried about how I would break the news to the team. I was embarrassed about this. I was a proud man and I couldn't accept that I had become a complete liability at a moment where the Secret Service needed me to get the job done. There are no backup pitchers in the Secret Service. They do not have the luxury of backup players at every position. If you failed to perform the mission, then someone else would have to pull double-duty to fill your role and the security plan is never as thorough when agents are overburdened with multiple responsibilities.

While thinking through a solution to get some help (I could barely move from the floor) and desperately trying to avoid being an unnecessary distraction, I had an idea. There was an agent assigned to the First Lady's protective detail named Bob who I had known from my experiences with Hillary Clinton's campaign for the U.S. Senate in New York. I met Bob during the Clinton Senate campaign when he was a new agent to the Clinton detail and he was now a senior agent on the Istanbul trip with President Bush's protective detail. I knew I could go to him for help without "stirring the pot" and causing a distraction. I called Bob, and despite him being bombarded with phone calls (Bob was the logistics agent on the trip and this was an assignment most PPD agents only did once due to the enormous workload and stress), he calmly listened to my story and he sent the White House doctor to my room. The doctor took a quick look after I dragged myself to the door to let him in and he immediately told me it was likely a severe disk injury and that resting it was the only solution. Both the doctor and I knew that resting it wasn't an option so he gave me some muscle relaxers for the night and something to dull the pain so I could finish the job I was sent to Istanbul to do.

The following day I awoke to a pain, which I had never felt

before, and this was with the painkillers coursing through me. Every movement, however slight, caused me to wince in pain. It took me an eternity to get dressed in my suit and every button on the shirt I was wearing felt like an electrical shock throughout my body as I moved my arm to button it. It was especially painful when I took out my issued P229 Sig Sauer firearm and placed it, with the two extra magazines, on my dress belt. The weight of it, with the heavy, Secret Service–issued Motorola radio we carried, just added to the downward pressure on my spine and when I moved they would bounce a bit. This was unnoticeable before, but now with the sensitivity of my back injury and the spasm that would not relent, every millimeter the equipment moved felt like I was being torn in a different direction then the one I was painfully trying to move in.

I met the other agents on the team in the lobby of the hotel and was not my usual talkative self, which they all promptly noticed. I kept an uncomfortable grin on my face to hide the pain, and we loaded up in the minivans the PPD advance agents had rented to transport the team around the locked-down city, and left for the first location. I would be a post-stander that day for First Lady Laura Bush's visit to the Blue Mosque in Istanbul. Compounding the already difficult and dangerous assignment (because, with the First Lady, we didn't have all of the assets that the President had) was the demand that we all take off our shoes while inside the mosque. I had never been inside a mosque before and was unfamiliar with the requirement to remove shoes, but the act I was putting on to hide the pain was now up. The agents at the site with me saw that I couldn't bend over to untie my shoes, and when I told them what was wrong, they quickly helped. I knew I was now causing more problems than I was solving by being there at the mosque. Determined to prove my worth, I stood my post at the entrance to the mosque, with no shoes on and in severe pain, until the First Lady left. The pain was a small price to pay to retain the dignity of knowing that I hadn't given up on the team. Giving up on the team is the unforgivable sin.

After the visit had concluded and President Bush went "wheels up" from Istanbul, Bob arranged for me to fly home on the support plane (the support plane was a backup plane from the Army Air Force's fleet of planes used as *Air Force One* when the President is aboard) because he knew it would arrive at Joint Base Andrews faster than the C-5 military plane I had flown into Istanbul on. On the trip home I was disappointed in myself. I had shown weakness. I had let the team down by costing them valuable time and effort to deal with my problems when the larger mission was far more important. Many reading this, who have been part of a competitive sports team, a branch of our military, a law enforcement unit, or a competitive business team know exactly what I am talking about. You *do not* let down "the team." But many others do not. This is one of the core reasons I feel President Obama is seen as out-of-touch by so many. President Obama doesn't seem to mind letting down the team and, I believe, he has a difficult time even understanding what "the team" is. I understand that there are those who will view any critique of President Obama as grounded in some implicit or explicit racism, and I do not deny that this exists with some people. But throughout my three years of political campaigning, and my time behind the curtain in the Secret Service, I feel these largely spurious charges to be grossly misguided and the attempted deflection to be unhelpful to the President and his party. It's difficult to shape and mold your future behavior from the clay of your past mistakes when you deny that those past mistakes exist and President Obama rarely acknowledges his errors.

Due to President Obama's failure to comprehend "the team," the President, and many of his media supporters, still fail to recognize why the Bowe Bergdahl incident and the Benghazi terror attacks are important issues to many Americans. They cannot understand, and failed to understand in advance, why these two scandals would be so devastating to them and would persist as they have. I knocked on thousands of doors during my congressional campaign and these two issues, whenever they came up, were always talked about with an unmistakable passion and fury. The people who found these incidents most offensive were typically military personnel, their spouses, and law enforcement officers. I understood why but I'm not sure, even now, that President Obama does. These men and women live by a code. That code states that the team comes first and that your individual responsibility is to do your job and make sure the mission is accomplished, no matter what. You *never* abandon the team. And, in return, for your committed efforts, you will *never* be left behind. Bowe Bergdahl left his men behind.

The swap of five hardened Taliban prisoners for U.S. Army soldier Bowe Bergdahl, who was alleged to have walked away from his team, deserted his unit, and abandoned his fellow soldiers, in violation of protocol, and potentially the law, by President Obama touched a nerve with many Americans who have lived by that informal code that views abandoning the team as an unforgivable sin. Compounding the situation were a number of additional factors. First, there was a leaked e-mail exchange between Bowe Bergdahl and his father, Bob Bergdahl, where he stated that he was "ashamed to even be American" and that "the horror that is America is disgusting." This type of rhetoric is foreign to the overwhelming majority of Americans who feel that America, despite its many faults, is a force for positive change in the world and that political differences are never an excuse to sell out your country. The e-mails led many to believe that Bergdahl not only abandoned his team in an active war zone, but abandoned "team America" as well. Second, Bergdahl's team was operating in a base in Paktika Province in Afghanistan and, after his disappearance, critical military assets were diverted from essential missions to search for him. Recovering Bergdahl became a top priority for the U.S. government in order to prevent the Taliban from using him as a propaganda tool. The resulting diversion of personnel to assist in the search has been cited as a contributing factor in the relentless twelve-hour assault, by over three hundred Taliban fighters, on Combat Outpost Keating near the Afghan town of Kamdesh. This bloody attack resulted in the deaths of eight American soldiers and the wounding of many others. Tragically, we can only speculate now as to what the outcome of this deadly battle would have been had military assets diverted to the search for Bergdahl been available to respond to the combat outpost sooner. We can only speculate what kind of lives the heroic American soldiers who perished and were gravely wounded on that fateful day, would have lived had Bergdahl not disappeared.

A common thread in most of the world's prominent religions is the importance of genuine sacrifice; the idea that your efforts and sacrifice, however painful and difficult to achieve, will result in a benefit to someone else. Bergdahl's actions were the exact opposite of a sacrifice and his team suffered because of those actions. Contrast Bergdahl's selfish act with the statements of Staff Sergeant

Clinton "Clint" Romesha who received the Medal of Honor for his heroic actions in the aforementioned battle for Combat Outpost Keating. Staff Sergeant Romesha, despite shrapnel wounds from the battle, exposed himself to enemy fire multiple times to support his team and he took the fight to enemy machine gun positions killing multiple attackers in the process. Yet, when asked about his sacrifice and his actions to fight for his team, he humbly stated, "I just didn't want to let my brothers down," he told *Stars and Stripes*. "I just relied on my training, remembered our lessons learned, and kept fighting for them."* Staff Sergeant Romesha clearly understands what "the team" is.

You never abandon your team and abandoning your team to join the enemy, as Bergdahl is alleged to have done, is an act so depraved that the many Americans who live by "the code" will never understand the motivations behind Bergdahl's actions. The President of the United States, celebrating this behavior with a White House Rose Garden ceremony with Bergdahl's parents, while pulling the wool over the eyes of Americans with regard to the details of Bergdahl's disappearance, was a political act so disingenuous and misguided that the White House staff member who thought of it should have been fired on the spot. I can imagine how disgusted the Secret Service agents and brave military and law enforcement men and women, who willingly put themselves in danger zones and risk their lives to ensure that President Obama can freely engage in continued, naked political gamesmanship, are with the President knowing that he honors dishonorable behavior, which violates "the code."

---

*Leo Shane III, "Army veteran Clinton Romesha receives Medal of Honor for Afghan fight," *Stars and Stripes*, February 11, 2013, stripes.com/army-veteran-clinton-romesha -receives-medal-of-honor-for-afghan-fight-1.207463.

The same code is the reason why so many Americans cannot forget the 2012 terror attacks in Benghazi. President Obama and his hard-left supporters desperately want this story to go away, but the many people I spoke with during my political campaigns and radio appearances will never forget Benghazi until the one question they want answered, is answered: Why was *nothing* done to save the men who perished that fateful night? Leaving our men behind to die at the hands of deranged terrorists in an ongoing attack and then disingenuously claiming that a video was the cause of the attack is an unforgivable sin. This is a violation of the code that too many within the radical left refuse to live by. Their fatal political mistake is that they believe they can convince others to subscribe to their cowardly "the political ends justifies the political means" approach, even if it means abandoning our men and women under attack and then lying about it, and this is one of the more disturbing paradoxes of leftist ideology. This paradox, which defies a simple explanation, centers on the hard left's belief in collectivism and the value of the whole taking precedence over the sum of all the individual parts. Yet, the very code, which many of us live by, which prioritizes team goals over individual desires, but celebrates individual effort at the same time, is shunned by the hard left. The hard left simply cannot understand that "collective" results will only be achieved through a collection of individual efforts. Another problem for the hard left's definition of what "the team" is, is that it is not the same as what many Americans view as their "team." Those Americans living outside of the distorted Washington, DC, bubble live their lives and subordinate their individual desires to support their "teams"—teams consisting of family, church groups, friends, local clubs, and causes. Most Americans celebrate individual efforts and meritocracies because they realize that a team task cannot be accomplished without a collection of dedicated individual efforts. In contrast, the hard left does everything it can to diminish the individual by taking his money, his freedom, and his liberty and, by doing so, they take away his initiative to produce, create, and guide that invisible hand to a better tomorrow and destroying team America in the process.

The hard left's fundamental misunderstanding of "the code" and "the team" was also evidenced by their disillusionment and confusion over the incredible success of the Clint Eastwood directed movie *American Sniper.* The majority of patriotic Americans who understand "the code" and the personal sacrifices our military men and women make everyday lined up to see *American Sniper,* not because they supported or did not support the war in Iraq, but because they understand and believe in American exceptionalism and the American "team." Many of my Libertarian-leaning Republican friends, who profoundly disagreed with the Iraq War, were deeply moved by the movie because they know their ability to publicly express dissent about the Iraq War is a freedom, which is only guaranteed by the enormous personal sacrifices made by the men and women who are willing to die to defend it.

The hard left is incapable of celebrating individual efforts in their collectivist goals and policy wishes and their disdain for the subject of the movie, Navy SEAL sniper Chris Kyle, because doing so creates a dilemma they cannot overcome. The hard left views America, and by proxy its military, as a force for global collective inequality, and celebrating the sacrifices of a sniper in the U.S. military would force them to question that strongly held belief. In my experience, asking someone on the hard left to introspectively question their worldview and move past the talking points and bumper sticker slogans they use is tantamount to heresy. Anger and resentment is their standard response as they digest the fact that Americans do not see the country as they do. They will call you "bitter," "angry," and any other expletive or derogatory term they can, to avoid confronting the fact that their view of what comprises "the team" is not what the majority of Americans think it is. We are not a country of men and women eager to genuflect or bow at the altar of a big and controlling government, which diminishes individual excellence and performance despite the hard left's demands that we do so. The people who have historically sought refuge here in the United States and the founding fathers of this country were a different breed of men and women. They were risk-takers, they were warriors, they were entrepreneurs, and most importantly, they didn't bow before the altar of anyone, an all-powerful government included. I find it odd that the hard left, which professes to believe in "the science" on a number of issues, fails to see the science of genetics in Americans' resistance to be controlled. We have passed these genes down from the revolutionary generation through "the greatest generation" and the hard left's complete failure to understand the success of *American Sniper* is just another symptom of their disconnect between what they disparagingly call "flyover country" and what we call home.

President Obama and his hard-left allies will never understand "the code" because they will never understand "the team." He will blame the men and women of the Secret Service, who have pledged their lives to preserve his, for his failures both big and small without a thought to the code. He blamed the Secret Service for shutting down the White House tours during the government budget negotiations despite knowing that it was nonsense. He blamed them for his failure to show up at the *Charlie Hebdo* Paris march despite never asking the Secret Service about the security conditions on the trip. President Obama believes in the failed ideology of collectivism because he has never been in an arena where the code was required and abandoning that code would have stung. He was an academic and lived in a world where good intentions rule and bad results are irrelevant. He never had to charge ahead in battle, or walk into an abandoned drug den in the middle of night to find a suspect, subordinating his own fears, as those who live by the code do because of their greater fear of letting the man next to them down. He doesn't know the code. He only knows that sacrifices are to be made by others, to advance his cause, and to support his team, regardless of the devastation this tragic outlook causes. The only "team" that matters to the hard left is the one that advances their cause and the only cause that matters to them is your individual liberty being subordinated to their dreams of concentrated power.

7

The Future of Policing

If, as the 1979 one-hit wonder by The Buggles claimed, "Video Killed the Radio Star," then video certainly killed traditional policing. The now ubiquitous video camera in our cell phones, portable computers, and tablet devices, has enabled anyone at the scene of a crime or police interaction to become an amateur video journalist. I left the NYPD in 1999, right before the camera and video camera became standard equipment in the modern mobile phone, and policing was very different then as a result. I never had to concern myself, in an interaction on the street and in the course of my police duties, with a subject anxiously grabbing his or her mobile phone to record the incident. And while there have been a number of positive changes in policing as a result of the video camera revolution, some of these changes have the potential to be detrimental for both the police officers and the general public. For example, the debate about video cameras on police officers, which record every interaction with the public, has been framed by many as one where the public benefits from the additional monitoring. I wonder, having been on the receiving end of an unpleasant interaction with a police officer, and having been a police officer on the receiving end of an unpleasant interaction with a civilian, if the general public has really thought through all of the potentially negative outcomes from being filmed by a police officer's body camera every time you interact with him or her. What if you are recorded by a police officer's body camera and it is a case of mistaken identity (something that happens frequently from my experience in law enforcement)? Do you want a video of yourself sprawled out on the ground in a potentially embarrassing pose to potentially become the next YouTube viral sensation? Once the images are created, regardless of the chain-of-custody rules for the video, the potential for it leaking out into the public arena is substantial.

Body cameras and dashboard cameras have altered the way we look at policing forever. Training mistakes, tactical errors, violations of use-of-force guidelines, and the use of inappropriate language are all on display for the world to see when a police officer is on videotape. Millions of people can evaluate and second-guess, over the course of days and months, what took a police officer seconds to decide.

We are doing a disservice to the public and the police officers by throwing them into a surveillance environment like this and training them as if it were the 1980s. Law enforcement equipment and training has evolved over time, but unlike in the Secret Service, where they constantly drill into their agents how to take a bullet for the President, my experience with uniformed policing is that the training occurs in the academy and little else happens afterward. Most police departments have basic in-service training programs but you cannot realistically expect a man or woman who has never been in a street fight in their entire life to take a few weeks of control tactics in the police academy and then go out and be able to stand toe-to-toe with a street-hardened subject who has no intentions of being arrested. I once watched in disbelief as a preteen girl held two NYPD Emergency Services Officers (the NYPD SWAT team) off for minutes because she didn't want to be taken away. My point is not to disparage the officers who were having a tough time with the young girl; it's to make the point that adrenaline and stress can combine to create a very dangerous scenario regardless of the size or strength of the subject.

Looking at the video of the death of Eric Garner in Staten Island, New York, and reading the accounts of the Michael Brown and Darren Wilson incident in Ferguson, Missouri, we all need to keep in mind that although the outcomes were tragic, it's easy for all of us to sit on our couches and criticize the responses of the respective officers. Before we criticize the officers we should all ask ourselves, "What would I do in that scenario?" If you were one of the police officers at the scene of the Eric Garner incident and he insists on not being arrested, do you walk away? If you were officer Darren Wilson, and Michael Brown attempted to grab your firearm would you let him have it? I understand that these are uncomfortable situations to think of, and I also understand that the black experience in America with regard to law enforcement has been far different than any other group of people, but we should not jump to any quick conclusions about who was right or wrong in these police-civilian interactions without applying a standard of reasonableness. What would a reasonable person be expected to do if they were in the same scenario? There is no other group of people in America that has been subjected to the degree of institutional, government-sanctioned racism as the black community. I will never know what it is like to be forced to drink from a water fountain labeled "colored." I cannot imagine the indignity of legal segregation, and worse, human slavery. There are legions of black Americans living today who remember their interactions with law enforcement far differently than the law enforcement my parents told me about. I always tried to remember this as a police officer, but that cannot serve as a reason to create a dangerous situation for yourself and others by unnecessarily resisting a lawful police action. Bias exists everywhere in our society, but vast improvements have been made where we now live in a world where the open racist is the exception, not the rule. Bias exists in policing as well, but we can only measure the actions of a man, not what's in his head. We can only measure the observable actions of a police officer and if every interaction between a white police officer and a black subject, which has a negative outcome, is going to be attributed to implicit biases then how do we move forward? How can we repair police-community relations if we can watch the behavior of the subject in a police interaction, and we can watch the behavior of the police officer, but only the police officer is subjected to an impossible analysis of what was occurring inside of his brain at the moment?

So, how do we fix these problems? There are a number of improvements to modern policing, which have the potential to revolutionize police-community relations. First, we must pressure police departments to pay as much attention to in-service training programs on use of force, control tactics, firearms discipline, and situational de-escalation techniques, as they do to pressuring their officers to write summonses. I remember being a police officer and found that many of the supervisors were under more pressure to generate revenue through parking tickets and moving violations, than they were to ensuring our training met the highest standards.

I cannot think of a more effective way to alienate an entire community than to treat them as piggy banks and to constantly be forced to harass them for small parking and moving infractions. Revenue generation, at the expense of prioritizing training not only alienates the community, but it violates the inviolable rule of training; police officers will react in a stressful situation according to their lowest, not their highest, level of training. Fine-motor skills deteriorate quickly under stress and any training program, which doesn't take this into account, is bound to produce subpar and even tragic results. Tunnel vision through the rapid deterioration of peripheral vision and the oxygen deprivation from an increased heart rate are additional negative effects from life-or-death stressful situations. These physical effects of stress impair judgment and if police departments do not invest in, and prioritize, training under these stressful conditions, then we will inevitably see more incidents of police-public interactions on video, which make the public uncomfortable. This renewed focus on training may cost money, but how much more money are police departments across the country willing to pay for videotaped use-of-force episodes where they will undoubtedly lose in court and be forced to pay substantial civil judgments?

Second, police departments have not significantly changed their method of promotion and career advancement for decades. The U.S. military has a strong need for college-educated future leaders, with very specific skills, in their fighting forces so they have an officer's training program, which allows qualified candidates, after completing an extremely rigorous officer training program, to enter as military managers. Police departments should consider adopting this model. It is absurd that an NYPD captain looking to transfer to the Los Angeles Police Department would have to enter into duty as a police officer and forgo all of his or her on-the-job supervisory experience. I learned a lot about law enforcement, interpersonal interaction, stress management, and conflict de-escalation during my four years as a police cadet and police officer and even more during my twelve years as a Secret Service agent. It would have been very tempting to leave the Secret Service for a management opportunity with the NYPD within the uniformed ranks if it were available under this military type of recruitment model, but it wasn't. There is an entire world of police experience out there being wasted because of antiquated hiring practices, which are the norm.

Third, we must reevaluate our commitment to community policing. "Community policing," as we now know it, is often an overused term, which doesn't accurately describe what its original intention was. The purpose of quality community policing is to have familiar law enforcement faces, which regularly police an area and get to know the citizens, the "goings-on," the businesses, the community leaders, and the religious community. Understanding the pulse of a community, the social influencers within it, the rhythm of it, and the elected leaders can be invaluable information in a community crisis. Sadly, this doesn't happen regularly because officers in larger police departments (ironically where this is most needed) are frequently rotated out of assignments before they have the opportunity to imbed themselves in it and police officers, in this data-driven environment, are not rewarded for the arrests they don't make. Not every interaction has to be an arrest or a summons for a good police officer who can build up credibility in the community by *not* taking a law enforcement action at every opportunity. Sometimes a stern talking to, and the judicious use of personal discretion, is the best law enforcement approach.

But in this new generation of computer-generated statistical monitoring of policing, the pressure is on the officers on the street to "do something" (similar to the pressure felt by elected leaders in a crisis, even when "doing something" can make the situation worse). These computer-generated data models began in the NYPD under the administration of Mayor Rudy Giuliani and were known in the NYPD as COMPSTAT, short for "computer statistics." These models are excellent tools for monitoring and tracking criminal activity and nuisance behaviors, but they are not the holy grail of policing. Overreliance on these models, and the pressure to produce summonses, and arrests, which can be measured, may be contributing to the police-community divide by forcing community police officers to always "act" when discretion may have been warranted.

Finally, police departments need to reevaluate the discipline models for their officers. When I was an NYPD officer, it was a career death sentence to accumulate a "CCRB" complaint. The CCRB stood for the Civilian Complaint Review Board and citizens could file a formal complaint at any precinct to this board for any number of infractions, real or perceived. The problem with this system, and many others like it, is that for every bad cop they punish, they pull down some good cops with them. Unfortunately, many of the people we dealt with in the street learned to manipulate the CCRB system to their advantage whether the officer was guilty of an infraction or not. If these individuals had a reputation for filing CCRB complaints, they were largely left alone because, even if an officer was cleared of any wrongdoing, the complaint never really disappeared from the officer's record. While the public should have a credible and easy-to-use avenue to file a complaint about a police interaction where warranted, they should not have an avenue to ruin a police officer's career because they have mastered the system. When an officer is cleared of wrongdoing, then he or she should be cleared and the record expunged; if not, you are creating a two-tier system where those who know how to manipulate the complaint system are free to violate the law, and those that aren't are subjected to it.

The video camera has given us all an eye into the world of what today's police officers go through. A police shooting on video can now be subjected to the eyes of millions in seconds as they view it on social media, cable, and broadcast television. Police departments and political leaders had better take these developments seriously because, as we saw in the Michael Brown, Freddie Gray, Walter Scott, and Eric Garner incidents, police use-of-force interactions are no longer localized incidents. If policing doesn't evolve and the proper attention to officer recruitment, training, compensation, promotion, and discipline isn't given, then incidents such as these will have the capability to destabilize the delicate police-community relationship, which has taken centuries to develop.

8

The Bureaucrats Are Far More Dangerous Than the Gun Carriers

President Obama made the decision to return to Martha's Vineyard for a summer getaway in the summer of 2010. When the President made that decision, he inadvertently made the decision for me to travel there as well, although not for a vacation getaway, but for a security advance. I was one of the few agents on the Presidential Protective Division at the time who had completed enough lead advance work to be eligible to coordinate President Obama's planned visit to the island retreat and many of the other eligible agents were either away on vacation or on other assignments, so my number was up. Although the security concerns on the island paled in comparison to the concerns I had when I coordinated President Obama's trip to Indonesia, Prague, and later to an active war zone in Afghanistan, the logistics on the trip were a nightmare. When I received the phone call from the PPD Operations section, I was apprehensive because of the logistics complications of operating on an island with no landbridge. The trip had enormous downside and almost no upside. The President planned on staying on the island for an unusually long ten days and that meant that I would be away from my wife and daughter, Isabel, for over three weeks securing the island to our standards and coordinating the difficult logistics. My friend Tom was assigned as the logistics advance agent and this was an assignment that I'm sure neither he nor anyone else wanted. Everyone on the protective detail hated doing logistics for a presidential visit because it was tedious and sometimes extremely boring work. Most of us had joined the Secret Service to do the tough assignments and get "in the weeds," as we used to say, not to make airline reservations and make sure that the hotel we used had food available in the mornings for the early morning shift. Tom was a detail-oriented agent I had been through training with and his background in the financial industry, along with his merciless sense of humor, made him a perfect fit for this dreaded logistics assignment. Martha's Vineyard presented all kinds of logistical concerns, which were uncommon on other presidential visits. First, the island is only accessible by ferry and by air. There are no possible vehicle evacuation plans in the event of an emergency and no way to get Secret Service agents on or off the island in case we needed backup or we needed to evacuate. Second, the length of the trip made booking blocks of hotel reservations nearly impossible. We had to resort to spending ridiculous amounts of money to rent homes on the island; something I felt would raise some eyebrows in the media, but it was our only option. And, finally, the President had an "open schedule." Whenever the President had an open schedule that meant that the Secret Service, me included, did not. Because the President had no documented schedule for the ten-day trip, that meant that me and my entire Secret Service advance team and support team had to wait around all day in "stand-by mode" until the White House staff advance would tell us that he was either "in for the night" (meaning nothing else was happening that day), or we would have to scramble to arrange security for whatever location he planned on visiting with little notice for us to prepare.

Killing time on that Martha's Vineyard trip while waiting around to hear what President Obama's plans were going to be was, ironically, one of the more memorable moments of my career. I enjoyed sitting on milk crates and chairs in the spacious guest house garage on the property where the President was staying, with the big garage doors open, and sharing "war stories" with the agents on the detail. I had been on the President's detail for four years at this point and had been through a lot with the men and women on the Martha's Vineyard trip; they were my team. We would sit in that garage for hours and poke fun at each other's historical Secret Service misfortunes. I would throw some embarrassing story out there such as, "Remember that time Tom (different Tom) ate the tamale in the nasty seawater-laced cooler on the abandoned beach in Panama, and lived to tell about it?" Then someone else would tell some other story about me taking Hillary Clinton's motorcade on the longest route possible (by accident) to a wedding in Long Island and showing up late. Then, I threw a story out there that I would quickly regret. I asked the guys if they remembered the disastrous motorcade incident in Italy when President Bush's limo stalled in the middle of a crowded street and I noticed that the laughter immediately stopped. I wasn't on that trip and I wondered what I had said. A couple of the guys gave me that look—the look we have all seen when we are saying something about someone and that person walks up behind you unnoticed. As it turns out, I should have never commented on a trip I was never on because I didn't know the advance agents on the trip and the agent who had coordinated the motorcade for that visit was sitting right there in the garage with us. I was horrified. He was a good sport about it and I apologized profusely for being an idiot (as they found out later, the cause of the limo stall had nothing to do with the agent's work, just bad luck). I learned another valuable lesson that day; few people ever get into a bad situation by shutting their mouths when they don't know what they are talking about. When in doubt, keep quiet; the absence of a comment is not the same as a comment absent of information.

A few days into the Martha's Vineyard visit, we were all sitting around in the garage chatting up a storm when the White House staff advance told us that the President wanted to golf at the Vineyard Golf Club with, at that time, New York City Mayor Michael Bloomberg. My first notification whenever we received word from the staff about a "movement" by the President was to the Secret Service supervisor on the trip from the protective detail, but my second was more important; it was to the Massachusetts state troopers we had been working with. The two troopers assigned to the visit were the kinds of cops I had worked with during my time in the NYPD; tough, no bullshit guys who were funny when they wanted to be, and tough as nails when they had to be. I spent a lot of time with these guys and they could move mountains on the Martha's Vineyard trip with a moment's notice. After ensuring that the motorcade route was secure we loaded up the President and headed out to the golf course. Most of the agents on the detail hated doing the golf assignments because golf courses, with their dynamic terrain features (tree lines, hills, sandpits, roadways, open spaces) were extremely difficult to secure. Combined with the long, hot days and little access to support teams, they were despised by many of my fellow agents.

The President took to the course with his friends and the New

York City mayor and the first few hours were largely uneventful. I watched from the lead golf cart as the President and his team shanked away at a series of golf balls and I kept a watchful eye on the ground and the skies for any potential threats. Hours into the visit, the monotony of the long day was quickly broken by a radio communication into my earpiece. One of the agents who had been conducting the airborne advance on the trip broadcast to me that he was monitoring a potential air intrusion. These usually worked themselves out quickly when air traffic control made contact and told the pilot that he was in unauthorized airspace, but this pilot was not responding. The minutes felt like hours because the supervisor on the golf course with me was hearing the same radio traffic that I was and he was looking for an immediate answer from me in case we needed to evacuate the President as the plane closed in on us. I asked him to "hold on," knowing that he wasn't going to like my answer, but I had no choice. I knew based on the airspeed and direction of travel, that we still had time to move the President if the situation degenerated and the plane changed altitude. Numerous calls to the pilot were going unanswered and we were reaching the point where I had to make the call. I grabbed my radio and called out to the airborne advance agent to scramble the fighter jet we had on alert and to immediately turn the unidentified aircraft around and get it away from the President's location. I sent a team to interview this pilot after we determined where he was going to land and told them to report back later on what they found. I suspected it was a rookie pilot who had strayed off course, which was often the case, and we returned to the business of securing the final holes on the golf course.

When I returned to the lead police vehicle with the troopers in it, these two grizzled Massachusetts State Police veterans I had grown fond of were incredulous that I had just launched a fighter jet from my radio. I really didn't think much of it because we had a lot of interesting tricks up our sleeves in the Secret Service, but after four years on presidential protection, some of it had become routine. The pilot was lost, as I suspected, but as I received the news with the troopers, they were still amazed at the fighter jet launch. I suspect many people see and hear about stories such as this and believe that the U.S. government is an all-powerful, all-knowing entity. And, although the government does a lot of things right in the military and law enforcement arena, incidents such as this are relatively anomalous.

Whenever I watch a movie where a federal law enforcement agent and local law enforcement are portrayed, some federal agent character inevitably pulls out a badge, in a moment of conflict between him and the local, and the local immediately backs off as if the badge had some supernatural power. This is usually accompanied by overly dramatic dialogue and the federal agent saying something such as, "We're the feds, back off. We'll take it from here." If only it worked that way in the real world. I can recall many instances in my Secret Service career where I was assigned to do a presidential security advance and the local law enforcement in the town or city we were visiting said, "No, we're not going to do that." In one Midwest state we visited during a security advance for President Obama, the local police department basically told us to pound sound when we asked them to close a road in front of a hotel. The road presented a significant VBIED (vehicle-borne improvised explosive device) threat to the President and I was uncomfortable moving forward with the security plan unless we could convince the local police department to close the road. Their reasons for not wanting to close the road were reasonable. I remember one of the police supervisors telling me, "Listen, you guys are outta here in a few days and we're left behind to deal with all of the traffic tie-ups and complaints if we close this road." In the end I knew he had a point and we were going to have to find another way to secure the hotel and the road in front of it. We decided on random checks until the latest possible moment close to arrival and then we set up a "sweep" area to check every car that drove by the hotel while the President was in the location. The local police department was satisfied with our collective decision and this example is a small example of how localities and states should push back against a sometimes overreaching federal government.

The road closure incident with the local police department in the Midwest was not an anomaly. Every time a security planning conflict with local and state police departments occurred I remember thinking, "Where is that 'powerful' badge from the cop movies when you need it?" The hard truth about the federal government is that, despite its mammoth size, its bureaucratic bark is far more dangerous to you than its law enforcement bite. There are far more state and local police officers than federal agents and, strikingly, there are more police officers in the New York City Police Department alone than federal agents in the FBI and Secret Service combined. Although the federal agents I had the pleasure of working with were some of the most intelligent and talented people I have ever dealt with, the federal government is largely a law enforcement paper tiger in the absence of assistance from state and local enforcement. Even our Secret Service protection operations would have failed miserably if it weren't for the dedicated assistance of state and local police who have the manpower and local "street smarts" to implement the security plan. The real danger to the average American citizen from their government is from overzealous federal government bureaucrats at the EPA, SEC, FDA, the DoEd, and others in the alphabet soup of federal agencies who are targeting American citizens for their grievances with very real penalties. These bureaucracies have a power, which strikes fear into the hearts of Americans—the power to tie you up in litigation and drown you, and your business, in a pool of paperwork so deep that an Olympic swimmer couldn't swim out. Here are just a few examples of this type of behavior:

- The Environmental Protection Agency (EPA) has been fighting to reinterpret the clearly written Clean Water Act to expand their regulatory powers to such a degree that small streams, on your private property, may fall under their authority.
- The Securities and Exchange Commission (SEC) showed an unusual interest in JPMorgan Chase CEO Jamie Dimon, a Democrat, after he criticized the Obama administration's "constant attack on business,"* and unleashed a litany of investigations into everything from their hiring practices to trading practices.
- The Food and Drug Administration (FDA) recently finalized new rules ordering restaurants, and just about every other facility where pre-prepared food is served, to post detailed calorie counts of the food items they are serving, under penalty of a fine, despite the fact that this information is readily available over the Internet.
- The Department of Education (DoED) cast a regulatory net targeting the payment models of for-profit colleges and universities, in the Obama administration's continuing battle against

---

*Brendon Bordelon, "Are the feds targeting JPMorgan for criticizing Obama?" *Daily Caller*, November 1, 2013, dailycaller.com/2013/11/01/are-the-feds-targeting-jpmorgan-for-criticizing-obama/.

alternative education business models and bankrupted for-profit Corinthian Colleges forcing them to sell off their assets at a discount only a government regulator could demand.

Notice, with the exception of JPMorgan Chase who was investigated by the Department of Justice as well, these cases hardly involved a swarm of FBI agents in black tactical gear swarming businesses and homes. The heat that was felt by the individuals involved in these cases was generated by the fire of an unaccountable and ever-expanding government bureaucracy, which views your liberty and freedom as its gift and gets to redefine the rules at its convenience, not yours.

The government has other means of intimidation outside of the brute force of arrest authority to force its will upon an increasingly apprehensive citizenry who largely distrusts government. An early September 2014 Gallup poll* showed that only 28 percent of Americans trust the legislative branch of government, only 43 percent trust the executive branch, and a historically low 61 percent trust the judicial branch. In my experience knocking on doors and talking with voters, from both the Democratic and Republican Party, the reasons for this lack of trust transcend political party affiliation. The bureaucratic invasion into our lives, a few cases of which I mentioned, in conjunction with the Internal Revenue Service targeting scandal, the Government Accountability Office spending scandal, the crony capitalism misadventures of the poorly designed "stimulus" program, the Fast and Furious gun-running scandal, the Benghazi attacks and the "video" scandal, and others, have

---

*www.gallup.com/poll/175790/americans-trust-executive-legislative-branches-down.aspx ?utm_source=tagrss&utm_medium=rss&utm_campaign=syndication&utm_reader =feedly.

whittled away any goodwill our government had remaining, regardless of your party preference.

While this bureaucratic spiderweb continues to trap a growing number of Americans, the irony is that a number of people, committing very serious federal crimes, are getting away with it. In stark contrast to the images we see in the entertainment media where the all-powerful "Feds" track down the bad guys and always win in the end, the dirty little secret of federal law enforcement is that only a small percentage of people ever get prosecuted or even investigated for breaking federal laws. Frustratingly, the segmentation of federal law enforcement into an alphabet soup of federal agencies and the artificial walls and silos that have been built up over time between them makes cross-coordination between agencies more difficult than it should be. The tragic result of this overly bureaucratic, organizational mess is that a guitar company (Gibson) can be raided by the U.S. Fish and Wildlife Service and subjected to arrest and fines for importing "East Indian Rosewood" (according to an unusual interpretation of Lacey Act) in violation of our import laws, but a Bernie Madoff type of financial hustler can swindle people out of over $60 billion and, despite multiple SEC investigations, escape jail until his Ponzi scheme was no longer mathematically tenable. Imagine, in the private sector, owning a business where you felt no need to balance your priorities? How long do you think you could stay in business under these circumstances? This bureaucratic mess has caused the federal government to lose its sense of the larger umbrella mission (tracking down the real bad guys) because of the unnecessary and sometimes conflicting missions, and priorities, of its numerous component agencies.

When I was a member of a Long Island, New York, Financial Crimes Task Force as a Secret Service agent, I was frequently disappointed in how many serious investigations we had to turn over to local law enforcement because they didn't meet the federal prosecution "guidelines" put out by the local U.S. Attorney's Office. The way the federal prosecution process works is mind-boggling in federal law enforcement and it should shatter the myth that the all-powerful federal government is knocking down doors night and day looking for the bad guys. The process frequently begins with an investigative lead or tip from an insider source or someone on the street that has done business with your target. From there, federal agents can spend weeks or months putting in the investigative legwork to present to an "intake" assistant U.S. attorney who can either accept or decline the case. Some of these cases are denied on "blanket declination" because the financial losses in the case are not substantial enough and there are few circumstances where these "blanket declinations" can be overridden (its widely considered to be bad intergovernmental "politics" to complain to the U.S. Attorney's Office about your cases not being accepted for prosecution because the fear is that they will stop taking even more of your cases). Process that for a moment; a guitar factory is raided by the U.S. Fish and Wildlife Service for a seemingly innocuous violation of an obscure act few Americans have ever heard of, and even fewer Americans care about, but financial fraudsters, actively involved in criminal schemes to steal your money are allowed to run amok because they haven't managed to defraud enough people yet. Strange.

All of these investigations are being scuttled, and the criminals potentially go free, while the U.S. government wastes trillions of borrowed taxpayer's dollars on failed policies and accumulates unheard-of amounts of debt to finance a mammoth government bureaucracy that sends the "Food Police" from the FDA out to restaurants to make sure that the calorie counts of the pre-prepared foods are accurate. This is only allowed to continue because there is no incentive for it not to. Government doesn't have shareholders, in the business sense, who lose money if they manage the company incorrectly, and the incentives to lobby for change are drowned out by the power of interest groups.

This is not a new problem. Famed University of Maryland economist Mancur Olson, in his landmark book *The Logic of Collective Action: Public Goods and the Theory of Groups,** posited that concentrated interest groups (in the cases I have described, the management and employees of the individual federal agencies operated in their respective silos) have a tactical advantage over larger groups bearing a diffused cost. The costs of this federal law enforcement mismanagement are diffused among so many taxpayers that no single taxpayer has an interest in organizing the massive effort necessary to break up and reorganize the broken system. Olson's theory has been challenged by those who would argue that diffused "interests" have organized themselves over time in successful efforts to fight back against concentrated interest groups, but the cases I have presented have additional problems. Those additional problems are political.

Our alphabet soup of federal law enforcement agencies and bureaucracies all have patriarchs and supporters on Capitol Hill and within the executive office of the President, for a variety of reasons, and the costs to elected lawmakers of taking on an agency such as the FBI, DEA, or Secret Service, and, by proxy its lawmaker and bureaucratic patriarchs, can be substantial. The political capital that would be required to massively reorganize

---

*Mancur Olson, *The Logic of Collective Action: Public Goods and the Theory of Groups, Second Edition* (Massachusetts: Harvard University Press, 1971).

our entire federal law enforcement operation and massive federal bureaucracy would likely mean career suicide for any ambitious lawmaker seeking to scale the Washington, DC, political ladder as the forces lined up against him to preserve the broken status quo.

A recent example of this was reported by Walter Pincus in *The Washington Post*,* where he covered the bureaucratic struggle to streamline our nation's intelligence, surveillance, and reconnaissance (ISR) architecture. Both the production, and the consumption, of ISR are spread out among numerous agencies, under different departments, and with multiple missions. The duplication and waste are legendary and a well-known problem in the DC inner circle. Pincus quotes a 2011 GAO report in his piece, which briefly sums up the issue saying:

> [T]he GAO described the task force as not having "full visibility" into several budget sources that fund the Pentagon's ISR programs. The GAO said that "multiple organizations conduct strategic planning, budgeting, and data processing and analysis across intelligence disciplines in accordance with their own priorities." A year after the GAO report, with fighting in Afghanistan winding down, the House Permanent Select Committee on Intelligence said that the Pentagon "has failed to strategically plan for how . . . [ISR] investment relates to future requirements."

Pincus also reports that in the December 2014 hearings on downsizing and streamlining U.S. Army operations that Arizona senator,

---

*Walter Pincus, "It's time for some intelligent intelligence gathering in Washington," *Washington Post*, January 19, 2015, www.washingtonpost.com/world/national-security/its-time-for-some-intelligent-intelligence-gathering-in-washington/2015/01/19/1c6fa808-9da4-11e4-a7ee-526210d665b4_story.html?wpisrc=nl_headlines&wpmm=1.

and former Republican nominee for President, John McCain "sought consideration of 'the far-reaching negative effects' that would come from cutting anything at Fort Huachuca in Sierra Vista, Ariz. The critical element at Huachuca, McCain said, was the 'Army's unmatched leaders, capabilities and platforms in the areas of cyber-security, network communications, unmanned platforms and intelligence, surveillance and reconnaissance [that] are forged right here at Fort Huachuca.'"

The battle over fixing our broken ISR infrastructure is a cautionary tale for genuine government reformers looking to fix this broken system. It's incredible to think that since the problems with the system have been well-documented that the DC inner circle cannot get together the political courage to fix what we all know to be badly fractured. We are running out of time to fix them, we are running out of money to paper over our mistakes, and the threat level from terrorism and attacks by our geopolitical enemies is rising. Senator McCain's statements are not unique with regard to lawmakers defending government facilities within their respective states, but they do highlight the problem of a concentrated interest (Senator McCain's concentrated interest is in pleasing constituents in his state and getting reelected) with the diffuse costs (the relatively small cost to the individual taxpayers for keeping the facility in Arizona open) that make these problems nearly intractable to solve. All of us are going to have to take the pressure off of these lawmakers at some point with an acknowledgement that if we wish to fix our increasingly broken federal bureaucracy, and really transform our government into something functional and efficient, that there will be some short-term pain for nearly everyone. Some facilities will be closed and others will be expanded. Some agencies will be shuttered, and some federal employees will be moved, but the rewards in the end from streamlining and specifying the various missions our government undertakes, and from breaking down the massive silos and walls that have insulated government managers at the top from the consequences of their bad decisions will be substantial. The costs of government could be dramatically reduced, the tasks the government performs could benefit from increased productivity and effectiveness, fewer government employees could be better compensated for their work and provided with clear goals and standards for performance, and the taxpayers could learn to finally trust their government again as it meets, and potentially exceeds, expectations.

Highlighting the paper tiger of federal law enforcement is in no way meant to disparage the incredibly talented and dedicated agents that do the investigative ground work with, at times, limited assets. It's also not meant to encourage criminals to break federal law because the threat of prosecution is unlikely (it isn't, the local police departments will eventually track you down). But it is a harbinger of a future where I envision states pushing the envelope in defying the federal government and taking back the ability to govern and police themselves, until the federal government can fix its broken system. We are already seeing this process evolve as states such as Colorado and Washington defy the federal government openly with their legalization of recreational marijuana use, in defiance of federal drug laws. These states realized, and the precedent was set when the voters of the state approved the legalization measures, that the federal government had no real options to respond to this violation of federal law. What was the federal government going to do, send in a couple of thousand DEA agents to make federal arrests for stoners smoking a joint on the street corner? The states are realizing that their law enforcement policies and priorities should not be strictly focused on the interests of the DC bureaucratic class, but on the interests of their citizens.

In an era of twenty-four-hour news and a constant stream of information easily accessible on the Internet, the news of each of the federal government's failures to maintain an iron grip over the states as they progressively ignore federal laws and statutes they don't like has the potential to become epidemic. It's not just the law enforcement options, which are limited with the federal government, but the political options are limited, with regard to fighting the states, as well. Can you imagine a scenario where the sitting President or Congress tries to cut off billions in funds to the state of Texas because they refuse to comply with a new federal mandate? (They tried this in Florida in early 2015 with healthcare funds and they have created a political quagmire.) Good luck alienating millions of voters and forfeiting away your party's future if you were to even attempt it. This de facto secession was noted by former presidential candidate and former Texas congressman Ron Paul, in a February 2015 speech at the Mises Institute, where he said:

> The Fed is gonna end. There is going to be a de facto secession movement going on. The states are going to refuse to listen to some of the laws. We've seen tremendous success already with states saying to the federal government, "We're not gonna listen to you anymore about the drug laws." And they're getting out of it, and I think the American people are waking up to that, and as far as I'm concerned, the more the merrier.*

---

*Abigail James, "Ron Paul issues dire warning: Secession is happening," *Catholic.Org*, February 20, 2015, www.catholic.org/news/politics/story.php?id=58876>.

Our system of federalism was designed to give the states discretion to actively police and regulate, within the bounds of the Constitution, its own residents. And, local governing is best as it assures local accountability. It also enables the states to experiment with different models of both policing and regulation that either attract or repel people. Those models would be tested in the same way taxation models are tested, by either the exodus from, or migration to, those states. Devolving the majority of the accumulated DC power back to the states sounds like common sense, but explaining to a DC bureaucrat that an agricultural regulator from Wyoming probably has a better feel for the soil moisture, market conditions, and climate trends of Wyoming than he does, can be a fruitless endeavor because he has no interest in forfeiting away his bureaucratic power for nothing in return.

So we are left with this: the threat of bankruptcy if you find yourself on the wrong side of our massive government bureaucracy, which reigns through intimidation, and a largely paper-tiger series of federal law enforcement agencies, which allow some of the most serious criminals to run amok while petty crimes are punished harshly because the federal agency heads choose to not communicate among each other when there is an existential threat to their agency. The legalization of marijuana for recreational purposes in the state of Colorado in 2012 is a clear example of the paper tiger exposed and this was a de facto acknowledgment that they cannot fight back against even one state that organizes against them, no less a group of states fighting back on multiple fronts.

Speaking after my victory in the 2014 Republican Primary for Congress in Frederick, MD. *(Courtesy of Garth Phoebus)*

My daughter Isabel singing the National Anthem at our Republican Congressional Primary victory party. *(Courtesy of Garth Phoebus)*

Speaking with the local NBC affiliate after our 2014 primary victory. *(Courtesy of Garth Phoebus)*

Hugging my wife, Paula, in a moment of pure joy, as we took what we thought to be an insurmountable lead against my opponent Representative John Delaney, during Election Night 2014. *(Courtesy of Garth Phoebus)*

The agony of defeat as our once insurmountable lead in my 2014 race for Congress begins to slowly dissipate late into Election Night.
(Courtesy of Garth Phoebus)

Speaking to my friends, family, and supporters late into Election Night as we found out that the race was too close to call and would be decided by the absentee vote count. *(Courtesy of Garth Phoebus)*

My wife, Paula, my daughters, Isabel and Amelia, and me at Smokey Glen Farm in Montgomery County, MD. *(Courtesy of Garth Phoebus)*

My wife, Paula, my daughter, Isabel, and me after winning the 2012 Republican nomination for the United States Senate in Maryland. *(Courtesy of the author)*

The quadcopter drone that crash-landed on the South Grounds of the White House complex at approximately 3:00 a.m. on Monday, January 26, 2015. *(AP Photo/US Secret Service)*

President George W. Bush, former Colombian President Alvaro Uribe, and current President Juan Manuel Santos, standing in the courtyard of the Colombian Presidential Palace where, just five years earlier, FARC terrorists launched a mortar attack and killed twenty-two people. *(Jose Miguel Gomez/Reuters/Newscom)*

Secret Service agents "getting big" and using their bodies to shield President Ronald Reagan inside of the limousine, while covering shooter John Hinckley Jr. and preventing him from continuing the attack. *(Courtesy Ronald Reagan Library)*

President Obama and the parents of Bowe Bergdahl, who was alleged to have deserted his unit, and was swapped for five Taliban prisoners. *(John Harrington/Pool/Cnp/ZUMA Press/Newscom)*

During my tenure as a Secret Service agent I watched Code Pink protestors (pictured here behind John Kerry) utilize strategic protests, and the media, to leverage their relatively small numbers into a magnified political message. *(Olivier Douliery/ABACAUSA.COM/Newscom)*

9

Charlie Hebdo, Paris Terror, and Presidential Leadership

In Washington, DC, perception is reality and managing percep-
tions is a lucrative business for those who are skilled at it. I was
sitting at home on Sunday, January 11, 2015, just days after the
terror attacks at the offices of satirical magazine *Charlie Hebdo,*
watching cable news, and I was surprised to see the massive size
of the crowd marching in Paris as a response to the terror attacks.
Word of the march had begun to spread throughout the diplomatic
community days earlier and I was astonished to see neither President Barack Obama nor Vice President Joe Biden at the event. Having been behind the White House curtain for many years, and
having been a part of organizing last-minute foreign trips under
tight timelines, I was certain that this was a misstep as I asked
myself, "How could the White House miss this?"

Here's how the process works when the decision has been made
to send the President or Vice President to an event, such as the Paris
march. First, the White House advance staff will notify the Secret
Service's Presidential Protective Division of the decision to travel
to the location. Second, Secret Service agents from the PPD will

be notified that they have been selected to conduct the security advance and the logistics advance. Travel arrangements will then be made to immediately get the agents on the ground, due to the tight timeline (sometimes, if commercial travel cannot be arranged the military will give us a lift). Third, the Secret Service field office with jurisdiction over the location will be notified that the President intends on traveling to the location. The respective field office will provide a separate agent from their office, who is familiar with the location the President intends to visit, to assist the PPD agent in the delicate security planning. Fourth, the U.S. Embassy with jurisdiction over the location of the visit will provide personnel and logistics support to assist the White House and Secret Service advance teams in accomplishing their missions.

With that basic template in place the Secret Service can pull off a number of magic acts, in limited time, to make a foreign trip, under extremely tight timelines, successful. The incident with fake sign-language interpreter, Thamsanqa Jantjie, at the Nelson Mandela funeral, who was able to stand for a prolonged period of time, just feet from President Obama, thankfully, is a rare occurrence (vetting people such as this overseas can be extremely difficult because you are relying on the local government's databases for information, which can be notoriously unreliable). Personally, I think these last-minute foreign trips by the President and Vice President are a very bad idea and that the White House Staff could do a better job in trying to understand the difficult situation they place the Secret Service in when asking them to perform this security advance magic act on foreign soil, and with limited time. But I understand the political pressure cooker the White House staff is immersed in to keep the leader of the free world actively engaged.

I was part of a security operation relatively similar to the Paris march, with regard to expedited timelines, when I was assigned as the lead advance agent for the signing of the New START Treaty between Russia and the United States in April of 2010 in the Czech Republic. I had just returned, both sick and exhausted, from another difficult overseas trip and drove into the PPD Operations section on my day off to return the satellite phones and my diplomatic passport, both assigned to me for the advance. I walked into the office and immediately knew something was up because it was unusually tense with activity. The office was about the size of a large American living room and was congested, as just about every other office on the eighteen-acre White House complex was due to limited space, and clearly something was going on. The operations team agents were all on their phones and they were all holding the desk phones to their ears with their shoulders as they seemed to all be pointing frantically to each other to do something such as "Throw me a pen," "Write this on the board," or "Call Joe Smith!" I knew I had walked into the section at the wrong time. Then the supervisor of the section—who had the phone in his right ear, while writing with his right hand—managed to gesture to me with his left hand with the universal sign for "Don't leave." When the supervisor hung up, I handed him the satellite phone in an attempt to quickly get out of their way and exit the office but he said, "You'd better keep that, and your passport, too." He told me that the phone call he had just concluded was a notification from the White House staff that President Obama and Russian President Dmitry Medvedev were going to sign the New START Treaty in Prague Castle in the Czech Republic and that I needed to fly out immediately to conduct the advance. I had just returned home from overseas and knew that traveling overseas, again, was going to cause chaos in my home life. But it was clear that the supervisor in the operations section was not asking, he was telling. He was telling, and not asking, because when the President makes the decision to travel somewhere he is rarely, if ever, overridden by the security concerns of the Secret Service. Part of the job of being a Secret Service agent is to do trips like the one I was about to be tasked with in Prague and not to make excuses about why it couldn't be done. If we canceled the President's travel itinerary every time we had a genuine security concern he would never leave the Oval Office and the White House staff knew it. The Secret Service has to be extremely delicate when it suggests that the President cancel a trip because, if the perception develops that the Secret Service is "crying wolf" about security then, as I stated in the opening of the chapter, perception is reality. During my time as an agent I only witnessed one trip that was canceled because of Secret Service security concerns. The protectee wanted to travel to an extremely dangerous area in South America, which terrorists of Middle Eastern origin had been known to use as a training and logistics hub, and we all thought this was an obviously awful idea. It was not obvious though to the protectee, and after credible confirmation from reliable intelligence sources that we would likely return home in caskets if we took the trip, we took our case to White House decision makers who we knew would call the trip off. We were right, and to the chagrin of the protectee, the trip was canceled. (We paid for it later as the protectee refused to let it go and brought it up in the car for weeks.)

If President Obama wanted to make the trip to Paris for the *Charlie Hebdo* march, I assure you the trip would have happened. This makes even more perplexing the statements of White House Press Secretary Josh Earnest when, just one day after President Obama's "no-show" at the Paris march, he blamed "security precautions" for the snub. Tying himself further into rhetorical knots,

Earnest tried to rebut Fox News Channel's chief White House correspondent Ed Henry's query as to why President Obama was able to attend the funeral of Nelson Mandela on short notice, but was unable to attend the Paris rally by saying, "The difference with President Mandela is that there had been discussions that had been ongoing for, frankly, a number of years about the ceremony that would take place in the event of his death. And so there was a much clearer . . . a much clearer plan that was already in place that could be followed for executing that event on a short timeframe."* Regarding France, he replied, "[T]here was obviously nothing in place because I don't think anybody contemplated the kind of attack we saw in Paris."†

This statement by Josh Earnest was terribly offensive to me and many of my former colleagues in the security and law enforcement arena, and demonstrated a total abdication of leadership by the President of the United States and his pandering staff. How President Obama could allow the Secret Service to be thrown under the proverbial "bus" as scapegoats for his poor decision not to attend the Paris march, spoke volumes to me and many others about the character, or lack thereof, of the White House. The Secret Service, now placed in an unwinnable situation by a President, which Secret Service agents had proudly pledged their lives to, had to respond by stating the truth; they had never been asked about the trip!‡ Making this statement by Josh Earnest even more unbelievable was

---

*www.whitehouse.gov/the-press-office/2015/01/12/press-briefing-press-secretary-josh -earnest-1122015

†www.whitehouse.gov/the-press-office/2015/01/12/press-briefing-press-secretary-josh -earnest-1122015

‡"White House hit for using security as 'excuse' for no-show at Paris Rally," Fox News, January 14, 2015, www.foxnews.com/politics/2015/01/14/white-house-hit-for-using-secur ity-as-excuse-for-no-show-at-paris-rally/.

that the Mandela funeral was a far more perilous security scenario for the Secret Service because the security infrastructure
at FNB Stadium (aka Soccer City) in Johannesburg, and the detailed security advance planning that should have been done for a
state funeral of such a prominent international icon, had clearly
not been adequate. I have no doubt that the inadequate security
situation on the ground for the Mandela funeral was relayed to the
White House decision makers early on in the process and, because
President Obama wanted to go to the funeral, it mattered little.
The bottom line is that President Obama was determined to go to
the Mandela funeral, regardless of the situation on the ground,
and despite the warnings from the Secret Service advance team.
Contrast this with the security scenario on the ground in Paris,
France, during the *Charlie Hebdo* march. The Secret Service has
offices in both France and South Africa and the offices are located
in Paris and Pretoria, respectively. The Paris march occurred
just blocks away from both the well-staffed Secret Service office
in Paris and the U.S. Embassy in France. The funeral for Nelson
Mandela was in Johannesburg while both the Secret Service office
and the Embassy were located in Pretoria. Combine this information with the fact that most of the high-profile streets and buildings
in Paris had already been "advanced" by both the French security
officials and the U.S. Secret Service before, due to frequent high-
profile visits there, and it's obvious to even the most amateur of
security observers that the White House was lying about why they
did not attend the Paris rally. It certainly was not the security
arrangements and, in my opinion, was simply because President
Obama did not want to attend the event and did not anticipate the
bipartisan backlash at his poor decision.

Genuine leadership is not about always making the right call but it is about taking responsibility for the calls that are made. Disingenuous statements about your motives, which seek to place the blame on those who work underneath you in the management chain, are the most pernicious of statements of all if you are in a leadership position. These statements do significant damage because the men and women working for you have little recourse to fight back through the management chain, the media, or the power structure. Although the Secret Service protects the life of the President of the United States, it has little recourse to defend itself against his poor leadership actions.

Volumes of material on leadership point to a common theme: "Spread the credit for successes broadly and spread the blame for failures sparingly." President Obama, and his team, could learn a few lessons from this statement after his series of cringe-worthy attempts to blame the Cincinnati Field Office of the Internal Revenue Service for the IRS targeting scandal, the "video" for the Benghazi, Libya, terror attacks, and the Republican Party for just about everything else.

The Secret Service team, which I led in Prague, pulled off a remarkably drama-free trip to Prague, with limited time to do so, and President Obama signed the New START Treaty without incident. But what he and his staff didn't see were the many sleepless nights, the painful negotiations with the Russian security team over the placement of snipers and tactical teams, and the extensive planning that went into the de-confliction exercises the Russians, the Czechs, and I conducted to ensure that, in the event of an attack we weren't shooting at each other. This is an exercise, which will be repeated countless times by the men and women of the Secret Service who will just get it done regardless of the circumstances surrounding the trip. Maybe in the future President Obama will consider this type of dedication and loyalty before he shamefully allows his mouthpieces to blame others for his poor decisions.

10

The "Establishment" Versus the "Grassroots"

The frequently used terms the "establishment" and the "grassroots" do not mean the same thing in every state, county, or even every locality, which they are used, even though they are used promiscuously. These distinctions are extremely important to understand because overly simplistic statements about real or perceived battles between the grassroots and the establishment party insiders can lead to misallocations of time, energy, and financial resources to fighting the wrong battles. Learning how to fight back in the battle against the Washington, DC, insider class, in the absence of significant funding, requires the use of tactics and strategies, which bypass the traditional Washington, DC, gatekeepers. Some groups have learned to do this effectively and some have not. As a Secret Service agent, observing from within the confines of the Washington, DC, "bubble," I witnessed some of the tactics these groups successfully employed in bypassing the gatekeepers.

We were closing in on the end of the second George W. Bush presidential term and the crowds had grown smaller and much of the luster of the presidency had disappeared. This is not uncommon for a two-term president who has become all too familiar, but the ongoing Iraq War had taken an extra heavy toll on the President and his staff in terms of both public approval numbers and internal White House morale. Whenever I reported to work as an agent assigned to President Bush's protection detail, I would park on the ellipse on the South Grounds of the White House complex and walk the roughly two hundred yards to one of the many black-iron White House gates, which allow access to the complex. One of the most depressing scenes I witnessed during the closing days of the Bush administration was the endless parade of White House staff members walking out of the complex as I was coming in for an evening shift. The staff members would be carrying boxes of the items from their desks, out to their cars, in poorly packed and overflowing boxes. With the President's popularity low, no prospect of reelection due to term limits, and little political capital to cash in on, many of the members of the staff were leaving with a hard landing and either no job, or a job that didn't meet their lofty post–White House expectations. Watching their somber faces as they clumsily fumbled to use their knees and elbows to try to push open the heavy, black-iron White House gates, while holding onto big cardboard boxes of items that had decorated their now empty offices, was a reminder of how quickly you can move from the top of the mountain inside the DC circle of power, to the bottom of the valley.

Adding fuel to the fire of depressing, diminished, second-term presidential prestige was the seemingly ubiquitous presence of the "Code Pink" antiwar protestors at a number of our in- and out-of-town presidential visits. Code Pink always appeared to have a unique ability to fluster the President when he encountered them due to their tactics. Much of what I learned about the power of grassroots organizing and its ability to bypass the establishment DC inner circle and speak directly to power, I learned from watching groups such as Code Pink operate. Disregarding their message for a moment and purely addressing their tactics, I learned that the size of your group is not as important as the perception of the size of your group. I also learned that snapshots and sound bites are the two most powerful political weapons grassroots organizations have in their guerilla war against the DC insider elites. Regarding the perceived size of your group, Code Pink's tactics made it appear to the untrained eye that the group was larger than they really were. They accomplished this by ensuring that they never wasted an opportunity to be seen by the President, and his entourage, as he traveled around Washington, DC. It even appeared that they knew what side of the street to place their small, but vocal groups on (noticeably visible with their bright-pink shirts and handwritten signs). I vividly remember an "in-town" visit (Secret Service jargon for a visit within the immediate DC metro area) to Montgomery County, Maryland, where I was driving the presidential limousine and Code Pink had a small protest planned. It was a hot day and the sun was intense through the thick, ballistic front windshield of the limo, but even through my squinting eyes (I forgot my sunglasses that day), I could see the Code Pink group about two hundred yards down the road. Those bright-pink shirts always made them hard to miss. The relatively thin roads of Montgomery County and the short distance between the end of the sidewalk and the lanes on the road, made small, but visible, protests particularly effective in that area. The motorcade wasn't very large that day (the size of the motorcade is inversely proportional to the number of years the President has been in office as interest

in his presidency wanes), but it was large enough to slow the vehicles down and that two hundred yards from us to them took an
eternity to cover. That slow crawl toward the Code Pink group
allowed the group to acquire something that the wealthiest and
most powerful members of society have desperately tried to acquire
for more than two hundred years, unfettered access to the President
of the United States' attention. The group, whether by intention or
by luck, managed to station themselves at the corner where we were
going to turn the limo to approach the waiting *Marine One* heli-
copter, and they became more vocal as we closed the distance. As
we slowly approached the group we had to slow down to make the
turn, which lengthened their exposure time to the President. It was
at this point that they were no more than a few feet from the leader
of the free world and this is when their impact was the deepest.

I quickly glanced in the limo's rearview mirror and could see
that this small group had managed to bypass all of the institutions,
security, and White House gatekeepers, and whether they knew it
or not, they had spoken to the President directly through their protest. He was clearly bothered by them and I know he read their
signs. He had a look of frustration on his face indicating that, even
if for a moment, they had gotten to him. If you attempted to gain
the President's attention and accomplish the same goal through
traditional channels, such as paying to attend an expensive fund-
raiser and being seated near the President, you would likely be
expected to pay tens of thousands of dollars or more. Of course, this
is assuming you could successfully pass through the vetting processes for both the staff and the Secret Service. Code Pink saved
themselves the tens of thousands of dollars and accomplished the
same mission for free.

The successful grassroots strategy Code Pink used was the

manipulation of what I frequently heard some DC insiders refer to as "snapshots and sound bites." Groups with a flair for the dramatic, such as Code Pink, have mastered the art of showing up at congressional hearings, presidential motorcade routes, high-society soirees, and other places with a guaranteed media audience, and placing themselves directly in the path of the television cameras, and loudly interrupting the event at just the right time and creating the perfect snapshot and sound bite. The purpose of this tactic was best summed up by the Fox News Channel's president Roger Ailes when he stated, "If you have two guys on a stage and one guy says, 'I have a solution to the Middle East problem,' and the other guy falls in the orchestra pit, who do you think is going to be on the evening news?"* Ailes's quip later became known as the "Orchestra Pit Theory" and the tactic works.

As the competition for viewers among the growing number of political news outlets grows increasingly fierce, elements of visual and auditory sensationalism are frequently incorporated to grab and hold the viewer's attention, and the sound bite plays a crucial role in this process. Political news channels and Internet-based mediums have business models that are driven by a number of factors, but their primary interest, and their revenue models, are built around the number of clicks on their Web-generated stories or the number of viewers to their programs. And, although this can be subjected to the pressure of DC establishment power players (some insiders will try to leverage their influence on Capitol Hill and the White House to try and steer who can appear on the cable news channels and who cannot), it will nearly always be overridden by

---

*David R Runkel, *Campaign for President: The Managers Look at '88* (Connecticut: Auburn House, 1989).

the pressure to cover visually sensational events, which have a near-magnetic effect on our collective eyeballs. This is where the quick sound bite plays a pivotal role because it can be played on a social media forum, as a teaser on a television news show, as part of a YouTube video, or another forum that doesn't require a heavy investment of the user's time and bypassing many of the DC gatekeepers in the process.

During both of my political campaigns, my team and I lived by the maxim, "If the message doesn't fit on a Wheaties box, then no one will remember it." In other words: keep it short and keep it catchy. The reasoning here is simple. The crowding out of traditional media communication channels by e-mail and social media has, in a number of ways, exchanged quality for quantity. Whereas a reporter, television producer, or radio booker used to call a communications director or a media representative for a politician or political activist to get a quote on a story, the ubiquity of e-mail has enabled nearly anyone running for any office or running any activist group, to send an e-mail to that reporter, producer, or booker and get noticed with a catchy sound bite or slogan. Any television or radio producer who has walked in on a Monday morning and had to filter through hundreds of e-mails from campaigns and activist groups can attest to the fact that many of them are deleted before they are even glanced at. If their attention isn't grabbed immediately, typically by the subject line of the e-mail, you will likely become a casualty of the e-mail recycling bin. Now, this is not a problem for well-established political commentators, in heavy demand, because they will be asked to appear regularly on cable and broadcast news, and to comment in online and print stories regardless of what they choose to release to the press. But it is a major problem for small and growing campaigns and activist groups lost in this avalanche of e-mail communications, and who are trying to develop that crucial name recognition, which is a political requirement toward advancing your operation's effectiveness. Keep it short, keep it catchy, or keep winding up in the recycling bin.

An illustrative example of the power of a punchy sound bite was Scott Brown's response to debate moderator David Gergen during the final debate against Martha Coakley in the 2010 Massachusetts special election for the U.S. Senate, a seat held by Democratic icon Ted Kennedy until his death. Gergen asked Brown:

> Mr. Brown, let me ask you this question, it's on a lot of people's minds. You said you're for health care reform, just not this bill. We know from the Clinton experience that if this bill fails, it could well be another 15 years before we see health care reform efforts in Washington. Are you willing under those circumstances to say, "I'm going to be the person. I'm going to sit in Teddy Kennedy's seat and I'm going to be the person who's going to block it for another 15 years?"*

Brown smartly refused to take the bait on the loaded question and quickly responded, "Well with all due respect it's not the Kennedys' seat, and it's not the Democrats' seat, it's the people's seat." Gergen later acknowledged to *National Review Online* that Brown, "stuffed me on that."‡ This quick, catchy reply, whether planned in advance

---

*Lachlan Markay, "Scott Brown to CNN's Gergen: 'It's Not the Kennedys' Seat'," *Newsbusters*, January 12, 2010, newsbusters.org/blogs/lachlan-markay/2010/01/12/its-not-kennedys-seat-its-not-democrats-seat-its-peoples-seat.
†Robert Costa, "Gergen: Brown 'Stuffed Me' With His Kennedy-Seat Quip," *National Review*, January 12, 2010, www.nationalreview.com/corner/192689/gergen-brown-stuffed-me-his-kennedy-seat-quip/robert-costa.

or not, received widespread media attention drawing both donors and invaluable earned-media attention to Scott Brown's campaign and, although it's difficult to gauge its effect on the race in isolation, few would doubt that it helped turn the tide in what would be an upset electoral victory for Brown against the heavily favored Coakley.

There are profound lessons here for grassroots groups and candidates seeking to bypass traditional establishment channels and getting their message to the people in power. The first lesson is simple, get out of the office and be seen (and get a photo of your team taken, remember the snapshots), but be seen in the right places, and at the right times. If you are out there with your team and protesting bad policy or bad politicians, or you are supporting a candidate, then you have to go where the cameras are, and the cameras are typically following the people in power, not those seeking it. The White House press pool, which follows the president, and the local political reporters, which follow state leaders are only human and they grow bored at times. I remember being assigned as the press pool Secret Service agent (the Secret Service agent who ensures that the press pool isn't infiltrated by potential adversaries) for the day on a series of out-of-town visits and watching them all grab their cameras and rush to the window to cover a loud protest just outside of the event. Many times the photos of the protest were the only coverage the President's visit received in the local paper at the expense of the event itself. As you stand out there and make your voice heard, you may think you are being ignored by the world's power brokers, but in my experience, they hear you, and the message has been sent.

Learning to speak in brief, easily remembered sound bites when dealing with the press, media interviews, and following the same

strategy in your e-mail and social media communications is critical. The best messages are those that sum up a narrative in a few short words or sentences. Nearly everyone remembers the strategic theme of the Barack Obama 2012 reelection campaign known as the "War on Women," but few people remember the tactical response to it other than Mitt Romney's "I have binders full of women" comment. Short and catchy works both ways, both for positive and negative messaging.

The terms establishment and grassroots (which are used promiscuously), at the state, county, and local level may encompass different organizational bodies and people, although at the national level there are some groups and organizations that seem to consistently fit under one of these labels, despite their occasional assertions otherwise. In Maryland, the statewide establishment, as I experienced it, is a small group of elected members of the House of Delegates and state senators who are aligned with a shrinking number of Central Committee members, a few of the county Republican clubs, and a very small number of lobbyists who, although it is a deep blue state, have managed to maintain friendships on both sides of the political aisle. The Maryland grassroots consists of the Libertarian wing of the Maryland Republican Party, along with a group of socially Conservative grassroots groups (some of which are comingled with Tea Party groups), a small group of former candidates, and activists, who have developed large followings, and a small number of elected officials who, by not toeing the party line, have developed political capital with the grassroots for their political courage. Friction between the Maryland establishment and the grassroots has followed a national pattern in states where the Republican Party is vastly outnumbered; when election cycle results are tough for Republicans, the squabbles

become public and vitriolic, and when the Republican upset victories occur and the party tastes sweet victory, there is a fragile rapprochement.

Maryland is a closed-primary state where the candidate with a plurality of votes wins and his or her name appears on the ballot under the party banner, unlike some other states, which select their candidates through party conventions. Closed-primary, plurality-wins states, select their party's candidates by the raw number of popular votes with no possibility of a runoff election, allowing any candidate who grabs the attention and loyalty of grassroots activists to win a low-turnout primary (which many are) by using old-school shoe-leather campaigning (door knocking, phone calls, parades, county fairs).

During both of my campaigns, I ran as an outsider to the traditional political process. The political gossip about me, among many of the political gatekeepers, that I consistently heard or was told about, was that I "didn't wait in line." This is a persistent and resilient theme, among those that control the levers of political power, who generally feel that moving up from locally elected office, to county, to state, to federal office is the only path toward making a significant difference in the political arena. Despite little evidence that this "waiting in line" process leads to more effective political leaders, or better policy prescriptions and outcomes, many elected officials, party officials, influential lobbyists, and interest groups desperately cling to this model. They cling to this for a number of reasons important to the survival of the status quo. The establishment's "wait in line" approach maintains the myth that there is a line and access to the "line" is only available through them. The ability to access the line, through the connected establishment class, comes with a hefty price tag. Accessing the "line" by obtain-

ing high-level establishment insider endorsements, and the transparent support, which accompanies it, is frequently viewed by the insider class strictly through the lens of: "How can I use this person later to obtain some future political gain?"

In many cases, the party insiders fear renegade types from their own party, to a greater degree than they fear their political party opposition because it upsets the delicate commodities trading in political favors business. Renegade types who represent the interests of grassroots volunteers, supporters, and small donors are free to vote according to the principles they ran on and that is an existential threat to the party leadership and the entire ability of the establishment to control who accesses the present and future levers of power and policy. Being able to corral elected members of their party, and their votes, in the halls of power and among the party officials within the party infrastructure, is the key to the insider class's ability to take collective action, even if that action runs contrary to where grassroots public opinion is.

Another factor critical to maintaining this "wait in line" approach for the establishment is that each rung of political power from the local, to the county, city, state, and federal level comes with a series of vetting processes that allows the establishment to maintain control over the levers of power. Potential renegades who vote according to their principles and against the establishment's interests, can be isolated and opposed at the early and local stages of their careers and their ability to develop a following, and influence public opinion, can be quarantined with minimal damage to the establishment's power structure. The establishment has an idea of who they want in specific elected offices, and party leadership positions, and they will not hesitate to run a primary opponent, funded by their aligned financial supporters and lobbyists, to take out a fellow Republican early in their career if they are a perceived threat. If you are lucky enough to garner enough of a public following in the very early stages of your campaign or your political activism, then they may employ other, quieter, strategies. Risking a rebellion in the ranks by openly opposing a popular grassroots candidate may not be an option and, in scenarios such as this, it's the sin of omission rather than commission, which is utilized as a strategic weapon.

During both of my campaigns, I was no favorite son to many of the party insiders and being left off of the speakers list for party functions became a regular occurrence. I was once left off of the speakers list for a Republican Party "Unity Rally" for winners of the Republican primary, held after the primary (where I was one of the victors), just a mile from my house, and despite the fact that I had the largest volunteer base and fund-raising operation in Maryland at the time. The event had a number of local reporters in attendance who refused to fairly cover our campaign and their biases about the seriousness of our efforts were confirmed when I was prevented from speaking at the event by members of my own party.

Learning to operate an effective campaign or activist group without the support of the establishment gatekeepers is a daunting task. A lot of energy is wasted fighting within your own party. At the federal level, groups such as the National Republican Congressional Committee, the National Republican Senatorial Committee, the Republican National Committee (who, unlike at the local level where the names and faces of the establishment frequently change, remain a constant in the establishment corner of the ring), can dramatically alter the terrain of a political campaign, and increase your chances of winning or becoming part of the "club," by simply throwing their support behind you in the form of independent expenditures in your race. These can take the form of call centers where volunteers can come and make get-out-the-vote calls, television, radio, and Internet advertising campaigns, or simply through introductions to influence peddlers. I cannot overstate the importance of these mechanisms of control and the influence they have on candidates susceptible to the trappings of faux flattery and access to power. Sitting in a closed-door meeting with a nationally known party or elected leader and being told how wonderful you are is typically the first step through the insider's door if you do manage to get elected. It resembles a grooming process in many respects and is tough to turn away. This grooming process is all part of the establishment power structure's methods for cashing in the favors for securing the votes for party leadership, legislation they need passed, leadership positions on committees (although the ability to raise money for the party is a larger factor), and most importantly, for crushing rebellions within the ranks.

Although I sat in many of these meetings I just described, I developed a small degree of immunity to the process through my many years in the Secret Service. A frequent site during my time as a special agent within the Secret Service, which forever tainted the way I looked at some of these political "celebrities," was the ease of which they lost their faux bravery in front of the President or some other person with substantial political capital. Some of the bravest political celebrities, in reality, are the first to cower in the presence of the President and others and when you repeatedly witness this, it is difficult to reimagine the mirage. This is not to say there are not some good people in powerful positions, and that I was above the process, far from it. I had many moments of weakness where I began to imagine what it would be like to be accepted within the ranks of the dictators of allowable political opinion and, although I was selective about the public battles I waged with them, there were many going on behind the scenes. This is the most important rule for operating outside of the national establishment's radar picture: pick your fights very carefully and only pick them when you have developed a support network large enough to be taken seriously. If you strike out publicly every time you are left off of a party press release, you are bypassed for a speaking invitation, or you are treated callously by an elected official or party insider, then this is a recipe for becoming an arsonist when you need to be a fireman.

Outside of being independently wealthy and having the ability to self-finance your own campaign, there are strategies you can use to run an effective campaign or activist group that do not involve the blessings of a massive bank account. As many successful and unsuccessful grassroots campaigns, as measured strictly by electoral outcomes, have shown us, a well-prepared, charismatic, unflappable, and passionate candidate or group leader is a near-mandatory requirement. Combine this with a strong message using the right sound bites and snapshots, a willingness to pick, and fight, the right fights, at the right time, and we can win the fight against the DC insider class.

11

It's All About the Money, but Not for Long

A mid-November 2014 Wall Street Journal/NBC News poll found that 56 percent of respondents agreed with the statement, "The economic and political systems in the country are stacked against people like me."* In my experience, those 56 percent of Americans are correct and, even if you disagree, you've probably heard the complaints about the corrupting power of money in politics. Money has, accurately, been called the "mother's milk" of politics. Whether it's wealthy individuals donating massive sums of money to candidates and organizations, or how wealthy individuals can use their own fortunes to buy an elected position for themselves, money can easily tip the scales against you. During my 2012 campaign for the U.S. Senate and my 2014 campaign for the United States House of Representatives, I was opposed by individuals able to finance their campaigns using their personal fortunes, one as an Independent, and the other as an incumbent

---

*James Freeman, "Americans Not Enjoying Era of Big Government." *Wall Street Journal*, November 20, 2014, www.wsj.com/articles/americans-not-enjoying-era-of-big-government -1416491970.

Democrat, respectively. I have no doubt that their abilities to sign a massive personal check to their campaigns played a significant, but not dispositive, role in the outcomes of both elections. Imagine sitting at your kitchen table two days before an extremely close election for Congress that could change your life, and that you have dedicated all of your efforts to, and discovering through a social media tweet that your opponent just allocated $800,000 additional dollars, to be spent over the final few days before the election, to ensure victory. I did not have to imagine it, because it's what happened to me.

I have vivid memories of Hillary Clinton's run for the U.S. Senate in New York in the 2000 election cycle. I was young, and extremely naïve at the time about the destructive relationship between moneyed interests and the politicians who seek favors from them. Having been raised in a family of JFK and FDR Democrats, I was surrounded by the Democratic Party's message. I heard the familiar "the Democrats are for the little guy" and "the Republicans are for the rich guy" lines and, although I was suspect, I generally believed there was some substance to it. That all changed with my involvement in the Senate campaign by Hillary Clinton. I quickly noticed that most of the homes we would visit with her and her campaign team were palatial estates with extremely wealthy owners and I began thinking quietly to myself, "Is this the little guy the Democrats are constantly talking about?"

One residence that stands out in my memory was a picturesque waterfront estate in the Long Island, New York community, of Setauket. I remember the residence not because of its massive size or its majestic waterfront views, but because of what happened to me while awaiting the arrival of Hillary Clinton's motorcade while acting as a Secret Service security advance agent in the front of the property. I was the "site agent" for the property, meaning that I was responsible for all of the security arrangements at the home and, as a result of the assignment, I had been there for a few days prior coordinating the detailed security arrangements with the homeowner. As the site agent on the day of Mrs. Clinton's visit, I was the agent in communication with the motorcade that was transporting her to the site and they were running a few minutes late. The homeowner, at my request, had instructed the guests not to park in the long circular driveway in the front of the house because I wanted to leave it clear for the incoming motorcade and wanted to be sure it would remain clear if there was an emergency requiring an immediate evacuation via the motorcade. As the expected time of arrival for Mrs. Clinton came and went, I was beginning to grow tense because the radio communication was spotty and we only had pagers to communicate with. The poor communication, combined with the late arrival time, made it all the more pressing that the entrance to the property remain clear to prevent the motorcade from being delayed any further. The moments began to feel like hours, as the normally busy Secret Service radio channel was dead silent. I waited and, as I waited, the internal tension grew as I began to wonder what had happened to the motorcade. I was still a relatively junior agent and my boss at the time, Marty, was a hard-charging manager who could be unforgiving when mistakes were made during a protection operation. This only added to the pressure to get this arrival right. Finally, I noticed something at the entrance to the property. In the distance I saw a black sedan and began to wonder if the motorcade had finally made it to the location. Confused, I thought to myself, "Surely the radio traffic would be clear if they were within eyesight," but I heard nothing in my Secret Service earpiece. The black sedan slowly made its way up the pebble-strewn driveway making that distinct light-crackling sound, as the rubber of the tires displaced pebbles along its path, and it quickly became clear that there were no cars behind it. Mrs. Clinton traveled around campaigning in a light brown, two-tone van the Secret Service agents jokingly called the "Scooby Doo" van (yes, we made up the name, not Mrs. Clinton, as her staff claimed shortly after announcing her 2016 presidential run) and, if this was the motorcade, then that wretched-looking machine would surely be visible by now. I stood there waiting for the mystery black sedan to stop at my location at the intersection of the circular driveway and the front door, and I reflexively held out my right hand in the universal symbol for "stop." (We held out our hand like this in the Secret Service to ensure the door where the protectee would exit the vehicle, lined up perfectly with the site agent's hand. In the event of an emergency this enabled the site agent to quickly signal to the agents in the car, and to the protectee, to evacuate before they even opened the door. Open doors are always trouble in the security arena as they introduce the protectee to an environment outside of the safe and controlled environs of the Secret Service vehicles.) The black sedan stopped at my extended right hand with its passenger-side front door aligned perfectly with my extended right hand. I didn't recognize the well-dressed occupants, but noticed that they were staring at me with a frustrated but confused look from within the closed and locked car. Now I was clear that they were in the wrong location and I began signaling to them using my hands to wave them on hoping that they would keep going and clear the long, thin driveway for Mrs. Clinton's motorcade, which was surely only moments away. Realizing that this brief attempt at hand communication was failing, I approached the driver's side door and heard the doors unlock. The driver slowly exited and, barely looking at me with a haughty half smile, he handed me the keys. He thought I was the valet. It was then that I realized that I was the "little guy" and that the wealthy and powerful see the world differently than the rest of us.

Context matters and in this case, a young man, in a suit, with his hand extended, and at an event with largely wealthy and powerful individuals provided all of the visual cues the driver of the black sedan needed to convince himself that I was the valet, and not a Secret Service agent. That this happened at a political event, and that similar events would happen to me throughout my career as a Secret Service agent, forever tainted the way I saw the intersection of money and politics. I harbor no unusual envy or animosity toward the wealthy due to these negative experiences because I learned much from them and viewed them as sociology experiments. The many meetings and dealings I had as a Secret Service agent with people far wealthier than I would ever be, and with far more power and influence, were invaluable in teaching me the "soft skill" of dealing with situational power asymmetries. I learned that there are two categories of wealthy individuals: there are those who are self-monitors and there are those who are not. Self-monitors have the ability to see themselves in a social setting as others see them. The self-monitors in powerful positions were the only people I could effectively negotiate with during a security advance because they didn't want to be seen by the advance team as overbearing or pushy and genuinely wanted the presidential visit to flow smoothly. Poor self-monitors didn't care much about what the Secret Service, or any other White House advance team members had to say about the presidential visit, it was going to be their way or it was going to be no way. I would simply have to placate these types of individuals and then make an appeal to a business partner or family member to plead for some flexibility. It worked nearly every time I tried it with the exception of those holdouts who genuinely did not care if the White House canceled the trip. (Yes, it happens; some people really do not care about the President coming to their home or business.)

The ability to raise funds to effectively compete in the political arena is a significant obstacle for the average American citizen interested in running for an elected office or challenging the political status quo. Purchasing television and radio advertising time in major media markets is one cost frequently cited as a barrier by many first-time candidates, but running a modern campaign is expensive for a number of other reasons unrelated to advertising costs. Having an experienced campaign manager, in the modern political arena of intricate data analysis, microtargeting, Internet messaging, sophisticated voter pattern analysis, and get-out-the-vote operations, are expenses no serious candidate can afford to forgo. Another series of factors are the personnel costs of a management team along with the office space and administrative costs of a well-run campaign, which can result in expenses nearly equal to the costs of a major-market media advertising purchase. These factors lead the average American citizen, interested in running for office, to a "chicken-and-egg" problem. If they do not have a wealthy group of family or friends to solicit for start-up funds to initiate a professional campaign, the personal wealth to fund the campaign, or they do not sit in an elected office, which they can leverage in their calls to potential donors when they ask for money, they can't get a credible campaign organization off the ground, which supporters will contribute to.

We are now living in a country where the government has grown so expansive that their imprimatur is required for purchasing health insurance, making alterations to your personal land, and even where you send your child to school. But it's this degree of control that government exerts over our lives that incentivizes the wealthiest among us to attempt to use their wealth to curry political favors to attain an advantage. Many of these wealthy donors may have passionate political beliefs, but many of them have a history of donating to whatever power is either in power or likely to be in power, regardless of their personal political preference. Political donations act as an access control mechanism for those able to give generously. Many of these business owners have been hurt by government regulators during the course of doing business and there are few things government bureaucrats fear (other than the elected officials who appoint them). Having express-lane access, through big political donations to elected officials, is one way of purchasing an insurance policy against big government intrusion. Standing at the entrance to the White House West Wing on West Executive Avenue is a front-row seat to the "access trading" that goes on at the highest levels of our government and the picture is not pretty. In just over two hundred years we have evolved from a country where the average American could walk into the White House lobby (ironically the reason the term "lobbyist" originated was to describe people in the lobby of the House of Commons attempting to influence lawmakers) to attempt to speak with the President, to one where you would be arrested and convicted for doing so without an invite, whose price is calculated in donations or votes.

Politics has sadly become two parallel universes in which the insider class and the average American exist separate and apart from one another. During my 2012 U.S. Senate campaign, a small business owner in the heavily Democratic city of Baltimore told a member of my campaign team that he would really like to host a fund-raiser for me, but when the information became public on our mandatory Federal Elections Commission filings, he was convinced that repercussions would result. He was not specific as to what those repercussions would be, but he hinted that he had been hurt before by donating to "Republican" political candidates. When you combine these intimidation tactics (real or imagined because the effect is the same) with the growing power of incumbency, and elected politicians creeping deeper and deeper into our lives, you have a recipe for a unidirectional flow of financial resources to the people in power. This flow of money toward those in power buttresses the status quo and makes the job of dislodging the political insider class nearly impossible.

During my initial foray into politics in 2011, during my run for the U.S. Senate, I was able to overcome the "chicken-and-egg" fund-raising problem through a fortuitous set of circumstances. Although luck was a companion of mine, and I was sure to work diligently to keep this companion satisfied, I took care to ensure that no opportunity was missed. Although my wife and I did not have the personal funds to quickly establish the financial credibility in our campaign account to warrant attention from the local and national media, we had a commodity no other candidate had ever possessed, although we were ignorant to the gravity of it at the time. I was a Secret Service agent who had resigned from the agency, during the Democratic Obama administration, to run in a deep blue state, as a Republican, against the sitting President's policies. I was naïve to the media implications of such a story and when I initially began receiving phone calls from local and national media producers to appear on their programs after my announcement of candidacy, I thought it was because former candidate for governor Brian Murphy, had agreed to be my campaign chairman, not because I was a Secret Service agent. The early media appearances on the Fox News Channel, CNN, and other channels, generated both local and national exposure and early money began to flow into my campaign coffers. This early media exposure allowed me to bypass traditional political gatekeepers at the local level, such as party officials and influential donors, and instantly establish that elusive, and hard-to-define, political credibility. This credibility feeds on itself in a positive feedback loop as the donations lead to more donations and more corresponding media coverage.

My story is the exception, not the rule, and luck is not a strategy for raising the money necessary to challenge the embedded political establishment. There are a number of strategies, and some larger macro trends, which can be leveraged that do not rely on vast fortunes, or luck, to run an effective political campaign or issues-based organization, which takes the fight to the connected insiders. There are numerous messaging opportunities that are free of cost, which can no longer be ignored. Social media platforms such as Facebook, Google+, Twitter, Vine, Instagram, and others, all offer opportunities to relay quality content to an audience at no charge. Establishing a social media presence and putting together a basic e-mail list is the first step to begin to generate campaign donations.

Many of the well-paid fund-raising professionals we interacted with were of little use in this fund-raising mission because most of them parroted the same line, "Get on the phone and ask for money!" When you are new to the political arena, as either a candidate, or an activist, cold calling potential donors almost always results in humiliation. The responses I received ran the gamut from "Who the hell are you?" to "Never call here again." I largely abandoned this approach after spending an afternoon in a Washington, DC, office with my former campaign manager and a consultant and, after calling nearly one hundred potential donors, and not receiving one donation, I ended the charade. This was a rude awakening after some early fund-raising successes due to the early media attention my campaign received. This is when I was forced to do what I should have done earlier, call my friends and family and ask for help.

Calling your friends and your family and asking them to financially assist you in what they may perceive as a quixotic political effort, is an uncomfortable experience, but even generating a few small donations from the effort can provide a morale boost to the campaign team. Many of these calls surprised me. People I assumed would be the most helpful, in some cases, were not helpful at all, while some friends who I assumed would be reluctant to help, became my biggest supporters. Another technique we used for generating early money was to ask local supporters and political club members to host free "meet-and-greet" events. While these events were free, it didn't mean that we could not ask for donations at the event. Convincing potential supporters to invest in me required a compelling presentation and we were always prepared to stay as long as we needed to in order to answer every possible question from a potential supporter. This wasn't easy because the schedule I kept on the campaign trail was relentless. It wasn't unusual to attend an early morning parade, an afternoon fair, a local activist event in the early evening, stop at the office, knock on a few doors late in the day, and to then attend a nighttime fund-raiser after the long day. I would be exhausted after giving my speech at these nighttime fund-raisers, but I felt that I owed everyone who gave their time, and showed up at the event, all the time they needed to ask a question or make a comment.

Gratitude also paid off for my campaign and, more importantly, for my feelings about the effort we were putting into our campaign. At the early stages of our fund-raising efforts, I made every effort to call every single donor, regardless of the amount of their donation, and thank them. I once spent an entire weekend sitting in my Chevy Tahoe, in my garage, calling nearly two hundred donors and thanking them for donating to a "money bomb" we put together. It was rewarding listening to the surprise in the voices of many of my $5 and $10 donors who, for the first time as many of them stated, received a personal thank-you call. It also speaks to the pernicious effects of a system dominated by the connected few and their connected friends that many of the people I called had donated before, but never received a call or a thank you. These grassroots donors are frequently lost in the donor pool among the wealthy few who receive all of the candidate's gratitude and attention.

On the Republican side of the political divide, it was the explosive growth of the Tea Party movement that showed the insider crowd that it's possible to raise millions of dollars from either a thousand $1,000 donors, or from a million $1 donors. The Tea Party's ability to bypass the financial gatekeepers of the old-guard establishment Republicans by crowdsourcing funds for non-establishment candidates is where their power has been the most pronounced. Many of these $5 and $10 donors giving to our campaign became $100 and $1,000 donors over time as they got to know me from my thank-you calls and my interactions with them on various social media platforms. A little bit of gratitude goes a long way.

One area where political newcomers (me included) frequently flop is in their acquisition of campaign vendors. When a campaign begins to slowly raise money and accumulate funds in the campaign bank account, they will inevitably receive a number of solicitations from various vendors selling a variety of campaign tools from voter-targeting tools, to apps, to robocall services. Like any other arena, there are really good, and really bad, vendors, and distinguishing between the two is one of the most important decisions a campaign can make. A poor choice in campaign vendors can bankrupt and sink a campaign quickly as they devour your bank account and produce little-to-no results. We had one vendor who was so ineffective that they posted pictures on our social media page with descriptions of a different event, even though the name of the event was in the picture's background!

The vendors that matter most for the fund-raising portion of political activism and campaigns, surprisingly, are not the fund-raising consultants. As I described earlier, I found most of their advice to be canned "Get on the phone and ask for money" nonsense. The vendors who really matter are those who can provide e-mail list building, and traditional mail fund-raising. Granted, many of these top-tier vendors will look at your Federal Elections Commission filings to ensure you are raising some money before they agree to assist you, creating another, smaller "chicken-and-egg" problem, but if you manage to raise funds from friends and family and smaller events, that should be enough to establish the necessary credibility. We raised most of our campaign funds, during both of my campaigns, from mail and e-mail vendors who were skilled at designing messaging and targeting donors likely to support a campaign such as mine.

Building lists of traditional mail addresses and e-mail addresses, is a tried-and-true method for building a grassroots base of financial support to fund your efforts and, although a network of quality vendors can lead your efforts in accomplishing these list-building goals, your grassroots team must provide the base to build on. Our campaign team rarely attended an event without a clipboard to collect e-mail addresses and home addresses from the attendees. The ability to grow these lists is directly related to your ability to generate funds without having to embarass yourself on the telephone cold calls. When your e-mail list grows to tens of thousands of names it's possible to raise thousands of dollars through the click of a mouse with the right message and not have to subjugate yourself to the humiliation of cold calls to potential donors.

Although money is still the grease on the wheel of politics, the information technology age and the growth of social media and ubiquitous e-mail communication has made the barrier to entry to politics easier for an outsider to overcome. Also, money raised from grassroots efforts on social media and through e-mail lists can be used far more efficiently now with the growth of targeted Internet advertising and the diminishing influence of expensive television advertising campaigns. The next generation of content will be broadcast to their audience from mediums such as Hulu, Roku, Pandora, smartphone applications, Web applications, and others. The ability to advertise to a smaller, and more targeted audience, on the aforementioned forums will further enable small, grassroots outsider campaigns to spend their limited financial resources more efficiently as they reduce "messaging waste" to consumers who are either not able, or not interested, in supporting them.

To summarize, technology has brightened the future for activists and potential candidates interested in fighting back against the political status quo, but not interested in paying homage to the establishment gatekeepers in the process. For most our country's history, prior to the 1970s, the most important election in the land, the presidential election, was largely determined by political party bosses in what could only be described as an "insider's game." This nominating process by political party committeemen set the tone for down-ballot races as well and political connections to both connected party leaders, and moneyed interests, were invaluable in determining which names appeared on the ballot. The post-1968 presidential election growth in both the prevalence of primaries, and the media coverage gained from primary victories, combined with the growth in Internet advertising, voter targeting, YouTube, e-mail, and social media has reduced the barriers to entry for grassroots activists and candidates. I see this trend continuing in the future as information becomes cheaper to obtain and easier to disseminate for both candidates and voters. These trends will never eliminate the power of money in elections, but they will reduce its influence.

12

Media Bias: Fighting Back

The hegemonic days of broadcast news and liberally slanted print journalism are coming to an end. The explosive growth in smartphone, and other transportable, technology has ushered in a new era of content delivery that will unbundle the delivery of news from its traditional overseers. Many of us were raised in an era where, if you did not hear it from NBC, ABC, or CBS national and local news outlets, you likely did not hear about it at all. The "it" you didn't hear about could have been a Conservative candidate, or a Conservative defense or refutation of a policy prescription. Podcasting, Conservative media Web sites, the live streaming of Conservative talk radio, and the delivery of daily content through e-mail lists are just a few of the mechanisms, which will continue to grow and provide information to an audience craving either an ideologically agnostic viewpoint or a Conservative one and, correspondingly, looking to break free from the trappings of the traditional media stronghold.

When you are a new agent to the Secret Service's Presidential Protective Division, you are typically assigned to the press pool.

The press pool is a group of reporters, writers, and photographers who are assigned to cover the White House. Following the press pool around all day, and watching them to ensure they stay "clean" (free of weapons or explosives), teaches the new agents to the President's security detail how to operate in this high-stress environment, yet it keeps them far enough away from the President to prevent any small mistakes they may make from heavily impacting the security plan. The press pool reporters, writers, and photographers are at the White House to cover nearly everything the President does or says. A few of them, whom I spoke with often, sarcastically called it "death watch" because they were there at all times to ensure that, if something happened to the President, their network wouldn't miss out on the coverage. Press pool members can rotate in and out over time as their assignments end, but some have been there for extended periods of time. I was never quite sure, based on my numerous conversations with the members of the pool, if it was the best assignment in journalism, or the worst. Their responses to the question, "Do you like working here?" were never milquetoast. They ranged from "I'm done with this" to "I can't believe I'm lucky enough to be doing this." Although many of the members of the press pool, who I dealt with on a daily basis, were very pleasant and professional to deal with, their politics were obvious when you got to know them, and many of them defied my expectations. I learned a lot about the media by working as the press pool agent, but it's what I learned about some members of the media after I left the Secret Service that altered the way I watched the evening news.

Although ideological media bias is a significant problem, it is not the only problem. Many members of the media simply evade or slant the truth, regardless of their personal politics, to garner as many Internet clicks on their stories as they can. One example, which I can personally relate to was the sensational, yet completely phony, December 2014, *New York Times* story* about the use of volunteer drivers in the presidential motorcade. The author of the piece Michael Schmidt, seemingly desperate to latch onto the click-bait gravy-train generated by the White House fence-jumper story, which had broken about a month earlier, wrote in the piece: "Volunteers with no special training are a link in the middle of the fastest, and highest-profile, chain of vehicles in the country. They are cheaper than the Secret Service personnel or local police officers who surround them on the road. And their cargo of lowly staff members and reporters is apparently less precious." This is a statement so devoid of analysis and common sense that Schmidt should have been embarrassed that it made it past the editor, but I don't think he was. I can't pry into his memory bank, but I assume he thought he had broken a major story about a pending danger to the President and rushed the story out without really thinking any of it through. First, the volunteer drivers in the presidential motorcade are not "a link in the middle" of the motorcade. Volunteer drivers drive the vans at the *end* of the motorcade and these vehicles have no direct role in the security plan. Second, it is irrelevant that the volunteer drivers are "cheaper than the Secret Service personnel or local police officers" because neither the Secret Service, nor the local police officers (who are paid by taxpayers), are authorized by the U.S. Code, to protect White House staffers and media members who fill seats in the vans and the press that ride along. If Schmidt is so concerned about the safety and

---

*Michael S. Schmidt, "Driver Wanted for Obama Motorcade. Novice Welcome," *New York Times*, December 25, 2014, www.nytimes.com/2014/12/26/us/politics/volunteers -get-license-to-drive-in-presidential-motorcade.html?_r=0.

security of his fellow members of the media, then Schmidt should lobby *The New York Times* to finance the training of a fleet of drivers to service them. In addition, Schmidt's comment about the White House staff and the press being "less precious" cargo are extremely disingenuous. Schmidt works for a major American newspaper, *The New York Times*, and as an employee of the *Times*, I find it hard to believe that he was unaware of this practice before he decided to write the piece. Notice when the piece was published: December 25, 2014. Notice anything significant about the publication date? The Christmas season is a notoriously slow news time and good material is hard to come by during the holidays. How is it that a member of a major media outlet, which has had members inside the "scandalous" volunteer motorcade for decades just discovered around the Christmas holiday that this was a major security threat worthy of his paper's coverage? This is complete nonsense. There are only two possibilities here. The first is that Schmidt knew about the volunteer drivers, considering his employer had its employees or associates in those vans, with those volunteer drivers, and he was desperate for a story and wrote it anyway. Or, he didn't know about the volunteer drivers, failed to do any homework, or even a small degree of background research on the story, and slipped it past an editor who missed it. There really is no other scenario that makes sense. This supposedly scandalous story is but one example of how the media can create a scandal at will and cost people both time and money, leaving nothing but reputational carnage in their wake.

As their audience slowly abandons the traditional media overseers, and turns to more ideologically diverse platforms, the old-guard media have been stubbornly resistant to admit their ideological bias and change their direction. Traditional print newspapers are hemorrhaging cash and many are either in bankruptcy or rapidly approaching it, yet they cannot seem to do the obvious; change direction! Circulation is decreasing at a geometrically growing rate and ad dollars, the foundation of the print media income stream, are drying up as ad buyers witness the industry's collapse. As reported by Ken Doctor, an analyst focusing on the economics of media:

> Put a few numbers together and we can see that newspapers take only about 8 percent of all digital ad spending, a share that's clearly in decline. In the old pre-Internet world, newspapers took about 20 percent of overall ad spending. Those two numbers are another shorthand method to understand the destruction of the industry's core business, as advertising once supplied 80 percent of the industry's revenues and nearly all its profits.*

Diversifying the editorial and reporting teams at these traditional media outlets would be an obvious first step toward attempting to reclaim some of their lost audience, but as I experienced during my political campaigns and during my time dealing with the press as a Secret Service agent, their commitment to a left-leaning ideology is a near-religious one that disregards the simple economic writing on the wall. When you decide to enter the arena of politics through either a campaign or as an activist, you must be prepared to deal with this ideological slant and the techniques and strategies biased outlets use to spread it. At some point during

---

*Ken Doctor, "The Newsonomics of Newspapers' Slipping Digital Performance," *Newsonomics*, April 25, 2014, newsonomics.com/the-newsonomics-of-newspapers-slipping-digital-performance/.

your campaign or your activism, you will likely find yourself in front of an editorial board of a major newspaper as I frequently did. Each time I sat down at the seemingly ubiquitous boardroom-type table, in front of these editorial boards, I clearly understood that the board members already had the answers to the questions they were going to ask me. Their endorsement determination was contingent, not on the evidentiary basis of my answers, but the degree to which I complied with their preconceived notion of what the answer should be. For example, while interviewing with a major national newspaper editorial board member regarding tax policy, I was dumbfounded at his resilience to basic historical facts on tax revenue, which any person with access to the Internet could easily verify. This board member asked me how the federal government would be able to raise the tax revenue it needed if, as I suggested, we lowered income and corporate tax rates. When I pointed out to him that vast amounts of easily accessible, historical data conclusively demonstrate that tax rates and tax revenues do not necessarily move in the same direction, he was apoplectic. He insisted that if the federal government were to lower tax rates on individuals, and American businesses, that the tax revenue to the government would decrease, despite any real evidence to support these claims. When I stated to him that a century of American economic data on the effects of tax cuts, under both Republican and Democratic presidential administrations ranging from Calvin Coolidge to John F. Kennedy to Ronald Reagan, provided conclusive evidence of tax revenue *increases* as income and corporate tax rates were lowered, he ignored me and continued with his questioning. What he failed to understand was that the question he was asking was not a valid question, when phrased as he insisted on asking it. A simple rephrasing of the question to "Why do you believe lowering the current tax rates is sound economic policy?" would have led to a healthy dialogue and the necessary exchange of ideas, which would have allowed him to make an educated decision about the quality of the candidate's ideas. Sensing the need to provide inarguable data to make my point, I refused to acquiesce to economic ignorance in an attempt to cozy up to this individual, and started a conversation about the 2003 tax cuts under President George W. Bush. Predictably, he responded about the damaging effects on our national debt that these tax cuts had caused and doubled down on his assertion that tax cuts cost the government money by claiming that many economists disagree with me. When I questioned who these economists were he said, "Paul Krugman." Krugman is a left-wing economist who, despite his Nobel Prize, has a number of deeply controversial left-wing beliefs about the role of monetary and fiscal policy in economic growth. I asked him if Krugman would argue the easily verifiable fact that the 2003 Bush tax cuts led to the largest four-year *increase* in government tax revenue in American history* and even offered to forward him some data on the tax cuts. Again, he moved on as if I had never spoken the words.

Unfortunately, the toxic interview with the editorial board member was one of many during my campaign where the pre-existing bias of the interviewer immunized him or her from factual data, which would confront and dismantle their left-leaning worldview. Dealing with this type of interview is not an easy task and some of the things we must do to fight back are uncomfortable but necessary. First, make sure you know the data, and are intimately

---

*Ryan Dwyer, "Dwyer: Bush tax cuts boosted federal revenue," *Washington Times*, February 3, 2010, www.washingtontimes.com/news/2010/feb/3/bush-tax-cuts-boosted -federal-revenue/.

familiar with the evidence you are using, to buttress your policy positions. Many of the reporters and editorial staff you may meet with have only a cursory grasp of the facts surrounding many of the prominent issues and, although they will challenge you, they are less likely to savage you in print if you can deliver a calm and collected, evidence-based case as to why your particular Conservative or Libertarian viewpoint is more likely to result in a successful policy outcome. Second, do not automatically accept the premise of a loaded question by jumping to answer it without challenging the premise of the question first. For example, an editorial board member at a local newspaper in the Montgomery County, Maryland, area asked me the loaded question, "How do you feel about reproductive rights?"

"Reproductive rights?" I asked in return. This could mean anything from the Affordable Care Act's contraception mandate to partial birth abortion, to my personal feelings about the use of various birth control devices. Although I could not read the interviewer's mind, it was obvious to me why he framed the question in the way he chose. He knew I was running as a Republican and his obvious Liberal tilt led him to group a number of disparate issues under the umbrella of a reproductive "rights" declaration. Asking him to clarify his question gave me the opportunity to discuss the nuances of each individual issue and prevented him from misquoting me as being against "rights" for women.

It's not just the prevalent ideological bias that stacks the media coverage odds against Conservative and Libertarian candidates and activists; it's the likelihood of getting any media coverage at all. Although I was lucky to have had numerous opportunities during my two political campaigns to appear on many of the national cable news channels and, in the process, to develop a strong national following, I was largely ignored by the local print media and many of the local news stations. Because of this media coverage disparity we frequently joked on my campaign that more people knew about our campaign in California than in Maryland. Making matters worse was that the standards for coverage continued to change. Staff members working on my campaign would release to the local press policy positions, appearances we would be making in their respective area, and successful fund-raising drives, and we were frequently met with a collective blank stare while they would cover my opponent's loose tooth. One member of the local media told me, in the early days of my U.S. Senate campaign when fund-raising was difficult, that he was not covering our campaign because "Money doesn't lie" and we weren't raising much. Yet, the same member of the media, when we consistently raised more money than my opponent in my subsequent campaign for the U.S. Congress, did not print a single story on our successful efforts. This form of media bias may be more pernicious in its effects on your efforts because whether you are running for office or trying to advance a cause, providing free coverage to tens of thousands of readers and viewers to Democratic candidates, while ignoring Conservatives, is an ideological subsidy, which is hard to replicate.

Fighting back against media blackouts is a difficult task because they have all the tools necessary to wage a print and television war while most of us have slingshots. Despite this, after a year of experience under my political belt, I came to the conclusion that my team and I had to fight back or we would be just another victim. The western portion of the congressional district I ran in was covered by a local paper called *The Herald-Mail*, and they were not fairly covering our campaign. They ignored us at every opportunity and it was hurting our efforts to get out the message.

Knowing that this was costing the residents of the area covered by
The Herald-Mail the valuable information they needed to make
an informed decision in the polling booth, my communications
director, Jim, e-mailed them a detailed account of all of the incidents of obvious bias benefiting my opponent. When we received
an unsatisfactory response, we sent the information to the team at
the Media Research Center and they published an online piece exposing *The Herald-Mail*.* After the Media Research Center piece
was published we began to see an uptick in the coverage to our
campaign, but the damage had been done.

There are a number of media outlets that do play fair and cultivating relationships with the television and radio show producers, reporters, hosts, and bloggers that control the levers of media
exposure, is a critical piece of the activist and campaign puzzle.
After numerous iterations, I learned that press releases and requests
for appearances should be crystal clear, they should present information from a yet-to-be-heard viewpoint, and the subject line of
the e-mail should effectively sum up what you want to say. The
subject lines of your e-mails should grab the reader's attention immediately, always being cautious never to step over the line from
compelling to salacious or from humorous to hokey. Whether
you are running a campaign or an organization, a media/
communications professional, along with someone with management experience with these types of organizations, are worth-
while expenses. Earned media exposure via talk radio or cable
news is invaluable for highlighting your cause, but keep in mind,
the men and women behind the media curtain, and who ensure

---

*Ken Shepherd, "Hagerstown (Md.) Herald-Mail in the Bag for Democrat in House
Race," *Newsbusters*, September 8, 2014, newsbusters.org/blogs/ken-shepherd/2014/09
/08/hagerstown-md-herald-mail-bag-democrat-house-race.

that the trains run on time, are solicited constantly, each and every day. Create compelling material that stands out, says something new, or says something old in a new way, and create a niche where you can provide subject-matter expertise in a concise television environment dominated by brief talking points and you are likely to get your day in the media sun.

Fighting back against ideological media bias does not end with debating techniques, embarrassing exposure for biased outlets, and sharp talking points. Many of these newspapers will publish well-written letters to the editor and this is an avenue, which Liberal activists have used to advance their point of view and you should match their effort by ensuring a steady stream of submissions. The significant growth in the blogging community can also help an outsider extend his message reach. Use your social media accounts to deliver high-quality content and ask your supporters to tag prominent bloggers, talk radio hosts, and activists and eventually, if the content is high quality, they may disseminate it to their audiences. This back channel can put your name and your ideas in front of a large audience, while bypassing traditional media gatekeepers.

13

Everyone Wants to Be the President and Here's Why

The presidency's allure resembles the gravitational pull of a political black hole, which is impossible to escape from. Few who enter politics do so without thinking, even just for a fleeting moment, that the path they are on will take them through the heavy black-iron gates of the eighteen-acre White House complex and into the Oval Office. There's nothing inherently wrong with political ambition, and the desire to scale the political power ladder, as long as the principles you claim to represent, and a commitment to service, act as your guide to the top. Unfortunately, my experience has been quite the opposite. Many of the political insiders I have crossed paths with want to scale the political ladder while stepping on your back. In Washington, DC, that ladder creates chaos because the decisions made by lawmakers are frequently made with that Oval Office sitting comfortably at the forefront of their conscious mind. Making the situation worse is that many of the members of the Washington, DC, political class are given a small taste of the power and mystique of the presidency during their tenures inside the DC beltway; just enough of a taste to make many of them want access to the whole kitchen.

Although no President will likely ever admit to it publicly the White House Christmas parties are a tedious set of affairs for the leader of the free world. I wrote "affairs" instead of "affair" because many of the attendees to these parties will say, "I'm going to the White House Christmas Party" as if there is only one majestic event for all of those lucky enough to be connected to the White House machine. There are a number of White House Christmas parties and each one is held for the different groups. The press has theirs, the staff has theirs, the Secret Service has theirs, and the First Family is free to add or take away these events as they see fit. During my time in the White House while assigned to President Bush's detail there were two Secret Service Christmas parties because many of the agents had to work while the first Secret Service party was going on. The Secret Service doesn't have the luxury of taking a day off because they have been invited to attend a party during their workday.

My wife and I attended a number of these events and, although she enjoyed them, and I always deeply appreciated the opportunity to attend, they were always work for me, and never pleasure. I cannot imagine the indignity of an agent unleashing his or her inner party animal while dancing on the State Floor of the White House in front of the White House staff and the First Family. The picture you receive as part of the event with the President and the First Lady is typically the highlight of the evening. This is the part of the event I imagine the President and the First Lady must despise the most. The Christmas party photo line operation they partake in forces them to stand in the Diplomatic Reception Room footprints, laid out on the carpet for them, for hours at a time. Regardless of the family or person taking the picture with the President, this is probably the highlight of their year, not the President's. It's not often that you have a few seconds to talk to the leader of the free world, even if the military personnel, ensuring that the line moves quickly, make sure that it is *only* a few seconds.

I remember bringing my daughter Isabel, only two years old at the time, and my wife to the 2006 White House Christmas Party and Isabel telling President George W. Bush in barely legible two-year-old English, "You're my favorite President." President Bush gave an avuncular laugh and my wife never forgot that, even if my daughter never remembered it. Although President Bush will never be able to recall the moment my daughter said those words to him, among the hundreds of thousands of conversations he had with supporters, I will never forget it.

There is some magical power to the presidency that is hard to adequately describe in words and, despite the fact that I worked with the President nearly every day prior to that Christmas party, the moment was still magical for my family. Members of the media and the Washington, DC, insider class will be hard-pressed to admit it, but they know exactly what I'm talking about. Admitting it removes the media's patina of impartiality and it removes the perception of "insider knowledge" within the insider class. I saw it often among insiders who pretended to be disinterested in conversing with or being seen with the President. In my experience there is an inverse relationship between the access a DC insider claims to have to the President, his feigned "disinterest" in face time with the President, and the access they actually have. Real insiders do the least amount of talking about how close they are to the President and aren't afraid to talk about what an honor that access is. But this magical aura around the president is very real and members of the Senate and House of Representatives see it when they have a brief moment around the President. They see the entourage, which carries with it an air of invincibility. They see the obsequious sycophants who hang on the President's every word desperately seeking an approving glance or positive comment. They want this, and they will do almost anything to get it.

The aura of the presidency is magnified by the accoutrements of the office and the Washington, DC, insiders, who witness it up close and personal, know it. The President has constitutional powers, but he also has soft power tools at his disposal to influence lawmakers who have yet to succumb to his policy wishes. Rides on *Air Force One*, rides in the presidential limousine, lifts on *Marine One*, front-row seats at a bill-signing ceremony, standing off to the side of the President's shoulder at a press conference, and joint rope-line handshaking marathons are all tools of presidential soft power, which can be used to cajole weak lawmakers into submission. These soft power tools work because a popular President can bring invaluable media attention to a lawmaker's campaign during the critical days and weeks before an election. In addition to the media attention it's the legions of photos and video images of a vulnerable lawmaker or candidate with the President that confer an elevated status to that person simply by being seen with the leader of the free world and the commander in chief.

Protecting the life of the President of the United States is an experience I am profoundly honored to have been a part of and getting a front-row seat to living history was a gift that becomes more valuable to me as I age and collect life's experiences. The presidency changes the people who occupy the office both physically and emotionally. A day in the life of the President is like no other experience on the planet. Although he pays for his own food (with the exception of official White House and Executive Office of the President functions), it is prepared for him and ready when he rises. There is a well-trained cadre of Secret Service men and women waiting to follow him from the moment he leaves his private quarters to the moment he returns and willing, at a moment's notice, to sacrifice everything to ensure his safety. His clothes are pressed and cleaned, his shoes are shined, his phone calls are even made for him as to avoid a misdialed number. He has twenty-four-hour medical attention by the military's best doctors, he gets his hair cut in the White House, he has his own gym, massage therapist, and even a pool, putting green, basketball court, and a bowling alley on the White House grounds if he chooses to use them.

The material comforts of the presidency are many, but the psychological comforts are more life-changing. Human beings are constantly seeking both verbal and nonverbal approval from others, whether they care to admit it, or not. There is an irresistible human urge to be wanted, to be admired, to be the center of everyone's attention, and to be powerful. The presidency satisfies all of these needs and wants with ease. Even in the worst moments of a presidency there are still people who would line up to interact with you for a brief moment. When you are the President of the United States, you are a piece of history, a chapter in a textbook, a portrait on a wall, you are not just the President of the United States, you are the single embodiment of a branch of government and a living piece of our American history. Absent Lyndon Johnson, every other modern President has sought to cling onto that power and the office with a white-knuckle grip. It is so desired that its pull on the political climbers in the DC insider class is unmistakable. There are only two types of people in the Congress and Senate, those who are thinking about running for President some day, and those who did, and have since given up. It is this gravitational pull, and the insider class looking to move past its event horizon and into its universe, that colors much of what our legislators do, or do not do, to sit in that Oval Office.

14

Your Vote Matters, but Not for the Reasons You May Think

You have probably heard about "big data" and its transformative effects on many components of our economy. But, have you ever heard about big data's effects on politics? The explosive growth in voter-targeting and data-gathering technology has created a class of what I call "super-voters." Many of these voters likely do not even know they are members of the super-voter class. How do you become a super-voter, and why is it distorting the political process, you may ask? This chapter will answer those questions.

During my 2012 campaign for the U.S. Senate in Maryland a knowledgeable campaign volunteer named Andrew would constantly remind me to make appearances at a retirement community in Montgomery County named Leisure World. Andrew understood what many office seekers in the state of Maryland who, during election season can be frequently seen coming in and out of Leisure World, understood; the residents of Leisure World vote in incredibly high percentages. The percentage of residents of Leisure World who vote are in such high numbers that Leisure World has its own voting precinct inside the Leisure World gates.

Office seekers are so ubiquitous in Leisure World during election season, and on election day, that even greeting voters there can be the equivalent of a political steel-cage match. During the 2012 U.S. Senate primary, I stopped at Leisure World on election day to say hello to some of the incoming voters. When I arrived, there was a line of office seekers from the board of education to the U.S. House of Representatives, all seeking the imprimatur of the Leisure World residents. I wound up at the end of the line of politicos, which meant that by the time the voter got to me, he or she had already been subjected to multiple rounds of "vote for me because" inquisitions and that they were approaching their redlines with regard to patience. Not wanting to upset the incoming voters who, as evidenced by the understandable "get away from me" looks on some of their faces after being nearly harassed by the conga line of politicos, were not enjoying this charade, I left early. Whether the residents of Leisure World were aware of it or not, they are supervoters and, although it is a label, which comes with a price (hounding by office seekers), it's a price worth paying.

The growth in data mining, or the ability to gather massive amounts of publicly available information on American voters, is changing politics and, in my opinion, not for the better. In the new Internet era, where information about you is bought and sold like a stock exchange commodity, online voter targeting and voter scores are all the rage. A number of companies, specializing in the online political arena, have devised proprietary targeting and analysis, which target and score voters based on a number of factors. Your social media profile, Internet browsing habits, the location you go online from, and your online purchase history, are all factors, which determine which political advertisements you see online, and which ones you do not. You're not just targeted, but you are scored as well. Some of the factors used to score voters are the voter's history of voting in both presidential, off-cycle, and local elections. But some voter data points that you may not be aware of are: your magazine subscriptions; memberships in groups, fraternal organizations, and political clubs; your donation history to groups and campaigns; and your publicly available social media profile. This information is plugged into an algorithm and a voter score is generated. In my 2014 race for the U.S. House of Representatives, I used a platform called Voter Gravity. In their system, voters were scored on a scale from 1–12 with 12 being a super-voter. A 12 score generally meant that the person it was assigned to would vote in the middle of a monsoon if the situation presented itself. Almost nothing keeps a 12 super-voter away from the polls based on the data. While this scoring system has been an enormous boon to candidates who, in the not-so-recent past, had to knock on nearly every door in a neighborhood to determine who voted and who did not (and even this information can be suspect because of a natural bias people have toward answering the question, "Do you vote?" with "Yes"), it has created an artificial divide between the super-voters in the neighborhood, and the rest of the neighborhood.

A number of political analysts and students of political science have racked their collective brains in attempting to determine why the divisions in American politics have become so stark. The "swing voters" in America are disappearing at a geometrically growing rate. "Crossover voters," who are open to voting for a Democrat in one race and a Republican in another race, on the same ballot, are a dying breed in American politics. Some have attributed this to the growth in cable news or to the gerrymandering of our congressional districts, where the political class attempts to make congressional districts "safe" for members of their own political party by stacking their respective districts with like-minded voters. While this may have played a role in the growing partisan divide due to its effect on political primaries (in a safe Democratic district, a candidate generally only has to win the primary, therefore they stake out far-left positions to pander to a small base of primary voters), I don't think it is the only cause. I am confident that the growth in the use of voter data has played a significant role in this process.

Put yourself in the role of a candidate, and you'll see why the data-driven campaign model's plays a vital role in determining who candidates interact with (a limited number of highly partisan voters). Party primaries to select nominees for the general election are, generally, very low-turnout affairs. The voters who vote in primaries typically have voter scores, using the model and scoring system we used, of between 10 and 12. Knowing that these are low-turnout elections, many candidates, who are limited on the time they can spend engaging in grassroots activities such as door knocking, will knock almost exclusively on the doors of the people who actually vote. This can have a dramatic effect on an election because as the voter base shrinks every vote you gain by speaking to someone on his or her front porch is worth that much more to the election outcome. Where this unintentionally widens the American partisan divide is that the candidate rarely interacts with anyone other than those who, although they may not support him or her in a primary, largely support his or her ideological principles in a general election. It is a classic case of not only "preaching to the choir," but preaching to the "choir conductor." With sophisticated online voter targeting dictating what messages you see online, and contributing to the "preaching to the choir" effect, it's a small wonder there are any crossover voters left at all.

Compounding the big data, partisan-divide problem is that,

even after the primary is over, many successful campaigns have followed the Obama campaign model and focused on persuading more members *of their own party to vote*, rather than convincing voters of a different ideological stripe to vote for them in a general election. President Obama's campaign team brilliantly employed this strategy in his 2012 reelection campaign and the tactic is spreading. The Obama campaign employed this tactic because their voter turnout data model demonstrated that it is more cost-efficient and time-efficient to target a low-voter-score Democrat (someone who occasionally votes, but votes Democrat), versus trying to persuade a high or low voter score Republican voter to switch teams in the middle of the game. It worked, and candidates, desperate to decipher the Obama electoral Rosetta Stone, noticed. If this trend continues, the only political preaching done in the future, which you will hear in the form of robocalls, texts to your phone, posts on your Facebook page and Twitter account, and knocks on your door, will be from a politician preaching to the choir conductor of the choir you sing in.

The growth in the use of big data in politics has not been all negative. Some of the effects are beneficial and, as these scores become more widespread, they will confer the "power of access" on a class of super-voters, which in decades past, was only conferred upon the political insider class. Access to elected officials, although they will insist otherwise, comes at a cost. Lobbyists, crony capitalists, and the power-hungry elites among us, figured this out generations ago. But as the data on voter behavior becomes more granular and fine-tuned, super-voters with high voter scores will become a force to be reckoned with, more so if they can coalesce into organized groups and use economies of scale to leverage their power.

I wrote earlier in the book about how perception in political activism is everything and I used the example of the tactical protest activity of the group Code Pink, as an example of a relatively small group, which used activism and protests to punch way above their weight class with regard to influencing the national debate. If groups of super-voters were aware of their voter scores, in a manner similar to being aware of one's credit score, and formed interest groups together, and employed some of the same tactics as Code Pink, their voice would be booming, and their influence would be incredible. Ironically, many of these super-voters are already combined together in groups in their neighborhoods whether they know it or not. For example, I got my start in politics by joining a local group of Republicans called the Severna Park "Elephant Club." I know many of the members personally and I am aware of their consistent voting habits. They are *all* super-voters and, if they were to master the tactical activism component, and get a hold of their voter scores to use as a metric-based influence weapon, then they could increase the decibel level of their voice in this growing political conversation. Knowing your score is important because it will increasingly work as a credit score works in a financial transaction. A person who is an excellent credit risk can use his or her score to get better terms in the transaction and a group of super-voters can do the same when "negotiating" with office seekers as to the terms they want.

Another benefit of voting often, being active in the local political scene, and donating to candidates and causes you support, is that your score will increase. While your individual vote may not swing an election, it will certainly increase your score. This is vital to you because, sadly, the growth in big government has sprouted tentacles, which wrap around nearly every component of our lives.

Whether it involves local zoning laws, state-based tax rates, or federally legislated Obamacare, the government has intruded into your lives at every level of organization. You *will*, at some point, need some assistance from elected officials in dealing with this growing monolith, and having a high voter score will greatly assist you in getting a lawmaker's attention. The score matters because the person picking up the phone in the office of the elected official you are calling for help can use that score to allocate the time of the elected official they work for. Based on a number of conversations I've had with elected officials at a number of different levels, this is already happening. Those callers to the office of an elected official that need help, and have a membership in an influential group, and a high voter score, will get the concierge service, while those callers for assistance who are at the bottom of the scoring chart will likely get left behind.

I saw this first hand during my 2014 House of Representatives race with another group that punched above its weight class. The group called themselves the "Sugarloaf Alliance" and they were residents of the congressional district I was running in. They lived at the base of Sugarloaf Mountain and they were fighting against the construction of a shooting range near their property. Leaving aside the merits of their cause, and focusing purely on their tactics, they were a model for civic activism and the power of people who vote and organize. My campaign was contacted by the group in the summer of 2014 and asked to support their cause and lobby the Frederick County local government (who had jurisdiction over the matter) to zone the shooting range out of existence. They were very well organized and they kept a detailed spreadsheet, which they conveniently e-mailed out to an e-mail list (which included elected officials), of what everyone they had contacted, including me, had done to help their cause. Not only did this let the elected officials know that they were watching them, but it advertised to office seekers what their opponents had done, or not done, for the Sugarloaf Alliance, creating a potential wedge issue for an office seeker to run on where it may have not existed previously. I researched the voter scores of many of their members and they were not bluffing; many of them were solid 12 voter score citizens. The shooting range was never built.

15

It's Not Just the Lobbyists
Destroying the Political Process

Our government has fallen prey to the trappings of concentrated interests and diffuse costs. Our Constitution limited the power of our federal government specifically to avoid the trading in favors. The rent-seeking behavior—which the Founding Fathers knew would become ubiquitous, if special interest groups with the means to pay for access to government power were also granted de facto access to the keys of the U.S. Treasury—has become a reality. Special interests are granted access to your money not only through the issuance of government grants, but also through the voluminous tax code. The ability of elected officials to use the tax code to grant Company A, a tax-code deduction not available, or easily utilized, by Company B, gives Company A a cost advantage in the new era of faux capitalism. If every other variable is held constant, Company B will generate a tax bill far higher than Company A, while producing similar products and, in effect, be driven out of business by their own government and not allowed to prosper in a free market.

Examples of our government "picking economic winners and
losers" are many. Whether it is the wind and solar energy industries, the ethanol industry, real estate, or a number of our domes-
tically produced agricultural products, many of these products
bear prices, which are not a reflection of how we value them,
but of how the government values them. The effects of this, com-
pounded over our entire economy, are devastating. Massive sums
of capital investment and consumption dollars are misallocated an-
nually in the United States to products, services, and investments
that are bought and sold because, although the buyers and sellers
thought the "price was right," the government ensured that the
"price was wrong." Prices are signals, signals that provide our
economy irreplaceable information and direction. The information, wants, and needs, of our more than 300 million citizens as
reflected in free-market prices for products and services, is simply
not replaceable by the limited information of government bureaucrats and elected officials. As I heard the Acton Institute's Reverend Robert Sirico state once in a speech he was giving in Colorado,
"It's not that government is too cheap, it's that government is too
stupid." Reverend Sirico was not speaking about the intellectual
aptitude or achievement of the people who work in government,
he was stating an axiom of resource allocation by price in a free
market, which places a premium on individual decision-making
across as many voluntary members of a potential free-market
transaction as possible. Limiting the decision-making through
government price fixing, and special tax-code deductions for those
with the influence and assets to pay for them, is a method of allocating resources by government force, not by consumer choice.

Unfortunately, it's not just the trading in economic favors and taxpayer financed handouts that corrupts our political process. There are other methods by which the costs to the businesses of those, with the means to buy access, are minimized at your expense. When I was a federal agent with the Secret Service, it was common for retiring managers within the agency to take post-retirement positions within the financial services industry. Although many of these men and women were highly intelligent and had impeccable resumes, they were not being hired for their ability to properly price a derivatives transaction. They were being hired because they possessed the most valuable commodity a retiring government employee can bring to a government-regulated business—"connections." While the problems with regulatory capture (government regulators who develop close relationships with the industries they regulate, which leads them to act in the industry's interest and not the government's) are well-documented, the problems with government employees charged with the investigation of specific crimes, then leaving the government to work for the very same industry are not. This can be just as damaging to the public trust. Time is an inflexible commodity, and if a government agent looking for a post-retirement job at a specific company takes the calls of the company first, the others will always be placed in a queue although they are taxpayers as well. Having the government law enforcement apparatus segregated into an alphabet soup of agencies, all charged with the investigation of specific federal crimes, contributes to this problem because if you do not "know someone" within an agency, which is charged with investigating the specific crime that you need help with, then you stand a good chance of being sent out in the cold. When I was a police officer with the New York City Police Department, I saw the opposite. The

NYPD is the dominant police agency in New York City and they have jurisdiction over the majority of criminal investigations. They do not have to deal with each crime being stuck within the "silo" of another agency, as they all fall under their umbrella. Therefore, if you do not receive proper assistance in your request for assistance, you can simply move on to another officer or a police supervisor. Good luck with that in the federal government.

I learned the "connections" lesson early in my Secret Service career when I dared to question a bank security representative who called our office seeking help. The man was rude and demanding and seemed more interested in telling me who he knew rather than what he needed and, although I regretted it soon after, I told him in the most diplomatic fashion possible to go pound sand. In minutes I received a call from the boss, who had received a call from his boss in the New York Field Office, ordering me to call the bank security official and apologize. I didn't do it, but I suffered for it later on as I wasn't given any high-profile cases from that bank for an extended period of time.

When you combine the witch's brew of highly paid lobbyists peddling influence, regulatory capture, and the hiring of government decision makers for their "connections," into a stew, you are served a plate of garbage, which the average American is being force-fed. With the U.S. government now consuming nearly 25 percent of our entire economy, the returns to investments in government lobbying have, in many cases, become far more profitable than investments in American businesses. While the amount of money spent on lobbying, which is reported on federal disclosure forms has recently leveled off, investments in other forms of lobbying have not. Much of the money invested in lobbying has moved underground. Whether it is referred to as "business development," "strategic communications," or "public relations," massive amounts of money are being moved into the shadowy world of the political-influence business.

The recent enhancements in the mandatory disclosure of lobbying activities has led to an arms race of regulatory arbitrage creativity that shows no signs of abating. Modern corporations can no longer afford to be on the wrong side of a misplaced political bet and this point has been magnified during the scandals of the Obama administration. One's individual political affiliation is no longer a shield, which guarantees protection against hostile political retribution from political bad actors, even in your own party. Jamie Dimon from JPMorgan Chase, a registered Democrat and previously an Obama supporter, learned this lesson the hard way after he dared to accuse the Obama administration of an "attack on business." A series of Department of Justice investigations later ensued at JPMorgan, one of which resulted in billions of dollars in fines. This is one of the many examples of what happens when you find yourself on the wrong side of the growing government monolith. The most glaring example of this activity is the infamous targeting of Conservative political groups by the Internal Revenue Service and the ongoing circus that resulted. When I served as a Secret Service agent on a financial crimes task force in New York, I had such a difficult time getting taxpayer records on subjects I was investigating that I figured out how to solve cases without them. We used to joke that it took the intervention of angels to gain access to taxpayer records. And, although I'm certain angels did not intervene in the Obama administration IRS scandal, someone did, and they managed to trade Conservative taxpayer records in a sick game of political stock trading. These scandals have not gone unnoticed in a business environment that increasingly relies on the permission of government officials for its continued existence. Sometimes the fear of government retribution is a more powerful deterrent than the retribution itself.

Another factor in the growth of the political lobbying business, and its shadowy underworld cousins, has been the availability of information on the Internet and the advancements in social media, which can take information and spread it virally. There are a number of Web sites that specialize in making information available about who is paying who to influence legislation and legislators. This was the kind of information that would require a trip to Washington, DC, and hours of painstaking research just a few decades ago. When combined with new disclosure rules, which codify what declared lobbyists can and cannot do, and who they must declare it to, the shadowy underworld of lobbying had the lightning strike necessary to awaken the Frankenstein monster. After all, why suffer publicly for lobbying on an issue if you can get the same job done behind the scenes?

Corporate money has been pouring into start-up companies full of fresh Obama administration officials more than eager to design "public relations" offensives through sophisticated influence-peddling schemes that, at least legally, are not defined as lobbying. Thomas Edsall describes one of these strategic offensives in a fascinating piece he wrote for *The New York Times* about the evolution of lobbying.* Edsall's description in the piece of the unexpected and rapid fall of the Stop Online Piracy Act, known as SOPA, despite an enormous amount of financial resources spent on "traditional lobbying" is telling. He writes:

---

*Thomas Edsall, "The Shadow Lobbyist," *New York Times*, April 25, 2013, opinionator .blogs.nytimes.com/2013/04/25/the-shadow-lobbyist/?_r=0.

In a month, support for SOPA imploded and with it the world of the expense account lobbyist. An anti-SOPA coalition abruptly burst on the scene towards the end of 2011 catching the SOPA backers by surprise. It included some high-dollar, high-tech corporations—Google, Facebook, Twitter, Yahoo—with the means to invest heavily in lobbying, traditional or otherwise.

Opposition to the bill quickly caught fire among the broader public. It was expressed in e-mails, text messages, voice mails, Twitter comments, Internet petitions, and outspoken attacks at town hall meetings—none of which have to be reported as lobbying-related.

The failure of SOPA is instructive for political activists and candidates because they don't have to rely on lobbying industry gatekeepers to fight back against the tidal wave of poorly designed legislation emanating from Washington, DC. Corporations are rapidly figuring this out as well as they withdraw money from traditional Washington lobbying firms and redirect that money to sophisticated public relations offensives. For this reason, it is crucial that the activist community and candidates spend time building and cultivating their social media presence. "I don't do Twitter" is no longer a valid excuse to forfeit away a communications forum, which costs you nothing but time. During both of my campaigns for public office, I communicated more often with people over the easy-to-use Twitter forum than I ever did with e-mail. Coordinated Twitter campaigns, where your group sends multiple tweets from the different accounts to politicians and media figures can have a deeper impact than these people might like you to believe. Many elected officials and media figures who operate their own social media accounts, will read some tweets directed at them, and if they do not read them, their staff surely does.

As I have repeated often in the book, it's not how large your group is, but how large your group appears to be, that matters. Having a small group or campaign with large social media followings, and learning how to coordinate a message to a media or political figure, serves the same purpose as the Code Pink protests along the President's motorcade routes, which I referenced earlier in the book—access. They bypass the expensive lobbyists, the thick gates keeping you away from the political players in Washington, DC, and the schedulers and political operatives whose primary purpose is to separate you from their political boss, and they allow you to speak directly to the person you are trying to influence. Bypassing these traditional channels of bought-and-sold lobbying communication to the political class is an inescapable step toward developing the grassroots influence necessary to influence better political outcomes and more responsible decision-making.

16

Why Blue States Matter

The Republican Party has no future. The demographic trends will lead down the path to a permanent Democratic governing majority." You've probably heard this before. I certainly have. While there is some element of truth to these statements based on the historical voting patterns of minority voters, along with the voting patterns of young, single, female voters, these trends, like many other historical trends, are only predictive of future results if you allow them to act as restrictions, rather than invitations for improvement. The Democrats' relentless focus on identity politics over principle and policy prescriptions, in conjunction with their media co-conspirators, has given them a tactical political advantage based solely on identity politics, and not on governing principles. If the Republican Party insists on staying on the defensive on these issues, rather than taking back the narrative, and telling the real story of failure, which Liberal governance has written in inner-city communities, then we will spend the next few decades apologizing, instead of winning elections.

The Republican Party "branding" problem in the minority

community smacked me in the face during my 2012 U.S. Senate campaign in Maryland. I was being introduced at a Baltimore event to a chorus of mild boos spattered with some polite, but subdued applause. I should have been intimidated by the circumstances I found myself in, but rather than cower, I was eager to seize the opportunity. I was running for the U.S. Senate in the deep blue state of Maryland, and we were just a few weeks away from election day and I had been invited to speak at an event called "Voterfest" at a historically black college in the city of Baltimore in front of a largely black audience as the Republican nominee for the U.S. Senate. I was excited to be given the chance to make the case for Conservatism and thought this was an opportunity to share its principles rather to shy away from the challenge. When I walked into the large college basketball arena surrounded by people seated in the stands in nearly all directions, I was impressed by the turnout. Based on the number of Democratic candidate tables displaying literature, which were set up in front of the large stage they set up for candidate speeches, it was pretty obvious that the small campaign team I brought with me was vastly outnumbered. There were long lines in front of the many candidate tables for the Democratic candidates, including the table in front of my opponent, U.S. Senator Ben Cardin, but foot traffic at our table was sparse. A few curious onlookers strolled by and, based on the stares and looks we received, they seemed more curious as to what possessed a Republican candidate to show up at this event, than curious about what issues I was running on. Despite the disadvantages and the tough political environment, I was determined to change at least a few minds. The Maryland Republican Party has, for decades, had no noticeable presence in the city of Baltimore (no Republican has been elected to the Baltimore City Council since the 1930s and before Baltimore's longtime Circuit Court Clerk Frank M. Conaway Sr. announced he was switching parties to become a Republican, in December of 2014, Republicans had failed to hold any office in the city since the 1960s), and, because of their absence, the Liberal narrative of the "evil Republican" was allowed to fester in the city, almost completely unchallenged.

While I was standing behind my campaign table, I listened to my opponent, Democratic incumbent Senator Ben Cardin, and the multiple rounds of applause he received, and I would look around at the faces in the crowd as he was speaking. As I stared into each individual face, I quietly wondered how the Republican Party lost each one of them. It was me who had grown up struggling in the city, not Ben Cardin, albeit a different city in New York. It was me who understood hunger pangs, money troubles, street violence, public transportation, and the power of a reputation on tough streets. I looked into the eyes of many of the people watching Senator Cardin speak and, although I didn't know them personally, I knew that look. I understood that stare and that search for an answer as to why their streets didn't look like the streets of American suburban utopia. I was sure Senator Cardin, although a decent man, didn't see what I saw, so how was I losing these men and women?

After Senator Cardin exited the stage, I was standing at the bottom of the short steps to the side of the stage, and they introduced me as the Republican candidate to a smattering of boos and some polite applause. I walked on the stage and grabbed the microphone and knew I had one shot. I opened by saying, "Thanks for having me. Did you know that the median family income in Baltimore City in 1950 was 7 percent above the national average. Did you also know that today it is 22 percent below the national average? Who did this here?" I was quoting an article I had been deeply impacted by, which was written by Steve H. Hanke and Stephen J. K. Walters in the August 26, 2011, *Wall Street Journal*.* There was nothing but silence. I was taken aback at how quickly the large auditorium quieted down. I didn't relent and continued asking why the schools in Baltimore neighborhoods were the worst in the state and what they felt the response would be if largely white, Maryland suburbanites sent their children to schools of the same caliber? Six years of graduate and undergraduate education in behavioral learning and neuropsychology taught me a lot about the inner workings of our complex human minds and I understood that years of associations, false imagery, and incendiary rhetoric about Republicans was only going to be overcome by a confrontational question of this nature. A question to the audience that was short, grabbed their attention, and most importantly, immediately confronted the worldview that had been thrown at them, was the only thing I felt would break through. I finished the speech to a loud round of applause and a long line of people waiting to speak to us at our campaign table and, although we did not have the campaign financial resources to compete on the Baltimore radio and television airwaves as the campaign progressed, I was proud of what we accomplished on that day and in our campaign in Baltimore.

Maryland doesn't have to be Texas, and Texas doesn't have to be Oklahoma, but charting a course toward changing the hearts and minds of black, Hispanic, Asian, and female voters mandates that each state play a role, even the deep blue states. Stopping, or taking a bold stand against bad legislation in deep blue states and,

---

*Steve H. Hanke and Stephen J. K. Walters, "How Property Taxes and the 'Curley Effect' are Killing Baltimore," *Wall Street Journal*, August 26, 2011, www.wsj.com/articles/SB 10001424053111903480904576510794280560566.

in the process, mitigating a legislative threat to a state's citizens is, in some blue states, the best political leadership a minority political party can provide. This matters to you, even if you reside in a red state, because organizing and investing in blue states can dramatically alter what happens in your red or purple state for a number of reasons.

First, the presidential popular vote matters, and the lack of investment in blue states leaves potentially millions of blue state, Republican popular votes on the table. Although the outcome of our presidential elections is determined by the Electoral College, we saw in the Bush versus Gore 2000 presidential election that popular mandates, expressed through the popular vote count, matter in the accumulation of vital, yet sometimes hard-to-define, political capital. Capital that is necessary and used up on the implementation of bold policy initiatives. We will never generate enough political capital to engage in education reform, entitlement reform, tax-code reform, and other stubborn political issues without a popular vote mandate behind us.

Second, as the primary season moves earlier and earlier in the calendar year; many blue states, such as Maryland, which recently moved its primary from September to June, can now act as political players in determining the major party nominees for the presidency in a competitive election. The past six years have shown us all the importance of a top-tier nominee for the presidency and the dramatic legislative penalties that come with losing the presidential election. The voters in blue states want to feel that they are part of our representative democracy as well, and disenfranchising them from the primary process is a guaranteed method for ensuring perpetual apathy in the blue state Republican ranks.

Third, as I was frequently told when I was boxing, "The best defense is a good offense." When you are punching your opponent in a boxing match he is worrying about covering up, rather than punching you. Investing in quality candidates running in difficult, but winnable, state and federal races within blue states keeps us playing offense and it prevents the other side from allocating both grassroots resources, and money, to candidates in red and purple states. When we divest national and state resources from blue states because we refuse to field a quality Republican team, Democrat Party volunteers and money simply move on to places such as Florida, Virginia, and Pennsylvania. In addition, this divestment prevents quality, principled candidates, and grassroots volunteers, from acquiring the experiential benefits of operating within well-funded, organized campaigns. Letting your "political bench" wither away due to a lack of attention is a silly strategy similar to a major league baseball team abandoning all of their minor league development teams. This may be penny-wise short-term, but it is certainly pound-foolish long-term.

Fourth, "What happens in blue states, doesn't stay in blue states." Blue states have increasingly become incubators for bad legislation, which metastasize into national problems. Whether it's misguided, non-data-driven, and potentially unconstitutional, tax and healthcare policies, which defy basic economics, actuarial rigor, and the wants and needs of their residents, states such as Maryland and Massachusetts have provided misguided national models for ineffective policy. Helping Maryland attain just six more seats in the House of Delegates would enable a future Maryland governor, Republican or Democrat, to veto bad legislation without the threat of an immediate veto override from the legislature and, in effect, stop bad policy in Maryland before it becomes a national problem.

Finally, and most importantly, the residents of blue states are not automatons collectively ready to universally subjugate themselves to an all-powerful, and ever-growing, state monolith. I love both Maryland and New York, both states that I previously called home. I was raised on the New York streets and, for a period of their lives, I raised my children in the Maryland suburbs. The ease of modern travel and transportation has incentivized residents of high-tax, heavily regulated blue states to move their homes and businesses to states with a more business friendly environment. But historically, Americans never surrendered their homes and fortunes to the whims and wants of either bandits or bureaucrats and fought back with a furor when their homes were threatened. Many blue-state residents do not want to leave their homes and are infuriated that government bureaucrats, and elected officials, have created the conditions where it may, eventually, be their only option.

Cede no more ground. As a prior resident of two blue states and now a purple state, America deserves better, and America doesn't end at the dividing lines between red and blue states.

17

Can the Current Two-Party System Save Us?

Frustrations are beginning to boil over. During both of my political campaigns it was not uncommon to walk up to a man or a woman, during a door-knocking session and get a hand in the face just as we made it onto the porch. Typically, the frustrated voter, as they were throwing me off of their porch, would say something such as, "I'm done with politics." Based on our voter affiliation data this didn't appear to be the sole domain of either political party because it happened with people we approached who were both Democrats and Republicans. The response is understandable given how elected representatives in Washington, DC, have failed to respond to the important issues dominating our time. Whether we find ourselves with a Democratic or Republican President, or a Democratic or Republican House or Senate, the problems persist and have largely grown worse, and the American people are waking up to this.

There are many reasons for this Washington, DC, dysfunction but the primary one is incentives. Politicians have little incentive to be honest with the general public because they do not want to be the one to tell the revelers that the party (no pun intended) is over. Honest politicians are typically out-of-work politicians because their opponents will simply continue to misrepresent the facts, lie to the voters, and win elections. Even more troubling about this situation is that many of the serious fiscal and monetary issues we are experiencing are solvable with a little initiative and a lot of honesty. Here are just a few examples.

The national debt continues to accumulate and is approaching an astonishing $20 trillion and, despite many in the media's, and their Democratic allies', assertions otherwise, we did not have a balanced budget during the Clinton presidency and we didn't have balanced budgets under either the George W. Bush or Barack Obama presidencies, either. The national debt rose every single year of the Clinton administration, an easily verifiable fact if one were to look at the government data on the matter,* yet many in the public remained convinced that President Clinton balanced our budget. The largest annual deficit, which added to our cumulative debt during the Clinton years, was $281 billion in both the fiscal years ending in 1994 and 1995, and the smallest annual deficit was nearly $18 billion in the fiscal year ending in 2000. At no point during the Clinton presidency did the U.S. government have a balanced budget or run a "surplus," contrary to the assertions of some in the media. Media acolytes love to report these stories in an effort to either avoid doing the basic investigative work or in order to continue their tragic love affair with the Democratic Party, facts be damned. I am a frequent guest host on both local and na- tional radio talk show programs and I am consistently bombarded by calls from Democrats and others who believe this Clinton me-

*www.treasurydirect.gov/NP/debt/current.

dia myth largely because they continue to hear it in the news. If you are confronted with this specious piece of bogus information warfare, ask the person one simple, yet irrefutable question, which he or she will likely not be able to answer: "If President Clinton ran a 'surplus,' then why did the national debt *rise* every single year of his presidency?" When President Clinton entered office the U.S. government owed roughly $4.4 trillion. When President Clinton left office the U.S. government owed approximately $5.8 trillion. Now, one doesn't need a calculator, or even an abacus, to conclude that $5.8 trillion in debt is greater than $4.4 trillion in debt. It's persistent myths such as this, which doom the Republican Party because they are forced to fight a fictitious enemy.

Annual U.S. government budget deficits were present in every year of the Ronald Reagan, George H. W. Bush, George W. Bush, and Barack Obama administrations as well, but I chose to focus on the Clinton years because if Americans are expected to unite behind a common cause, it would be helpful if our media would report fact-based data to help us make the tough decisions. They simply refuse to do this with regard to the mythical Clinton "surplus." Some honest reporting would be helpful, but it wouldn't absolve us of the tough decisions we have to make in the future. There is a coming tide of debt red ink about to flood our shores and we can't continue to ignore it. Neither Republicans nor Democrats seem willing to tell the American people what needs to be done. The federal government is currently spending so much taxpayer money, and future taxpayer earnings in the form of new debt, that even if we were to cut every dollar of discretionary federal government spending (government spending minus defense and entitlement spending) today, we would be still be running an annual deficit and would have done almost nothing to shrink our $18 trillion in accumulated debt. Where is the plan, documented and laid out on the table for all of us to see, which is going to solve this potentially fatal problem? Is a third political party the only way to force honesty and accountability onto elected leaders?

Let's take a look at another problem that a lot of honesty, and a dose of leadership, within either political party could fix relatively easily. Social Security is running on empty and has accrued obligations that, on its current funding trajectory, will make it insolvent by the year 2033.* Social Security's own Board of Trustees has clearly laid out, in its recent report on the actuarial status of the program, that the economic future of the program is grim.† American workers retiring in the coming decades will receive in return for their Social Security contributions, paid via payroll taxes, an increasingly smaller fraction of the earnings they contributed. None of this is news to the insider class of Republicans and Democrats in Washington, DC, but the Liberal interest group/ media coalition has people running for political office so terrified of speaking out on Social Security that we are now looking at the most predictable, largest, and avoidable bankruptcy in American history. This bankruptcy is a matter of mathematical certainty as certain as knowing the value of $3 + 3$ if nothing is done to reform the program. Yet, few have the guts to tell the American people the hard truth. Can you imagine a financial adviser selling an investment portfolio to the American people where they deduct the

---

*Rachel Greszler and Romina Boccia, "Social Security Trustees Report Unfunded Liability Increased $1.1 Trillion and Projected Insolvency by 2033," The Heritage Foundation, August 4, 2014, www.heritage.org/research/reports/2014/08/social-security-trustees-report-unfunded-liability-increased-11-trillion-and-projected-insolvency-in-2033#_ftn1.
†U.S. Social Security Administration, *The 2014 Annual Report of the Board of Trustees of the Federal Old-Age and Survivors Insurance and Federal Disability Insurance Trust Funds*, July 28, 2014, www.ssa.gov/oact/tr/2014/tr2014.pdf.

funds automatically from your paycheck, and where only they have access to it, and where it is absolutely certain to lose money over time? Sadly, these are the hard facts about a program that millions of Americans have come to plan their lives around and little has been done to solve the problem despite available and obvious fixes. Means testing, personal accounts, indexing the distribution of benefits to longevity markers, and other practical solutions are the only path forward, and I was always frustrated on the campaign trail by those who think that burying their heads in the sand is a solution.

These are but a few of the problems that have solutions, but do not have ambassadors to advance them.

Is a third political party the answer, given this failure of leadership? I don't think it is, for a number of reasons ranging from principled reasons to mathematical and tactical ones. On principle, we built the Republican Party. Grassroots volunteers and donors comprise the overwhelming majority of the party. It is their dollars and sweat equity that has built the e-mail lists, the data files, the brand recognition, the party ballot lines we have access to, the debate stage slots that come with a major party nomination, and other intangibles that would take decades of work and millions of dollars to credibly reconstruct through a third party. If a burglar broke into your home in the middle of the night, would you leave him the keys, take your family, and walk out giving him the house? Of course not, so why would you forfeit away what you built simply to start over again and later run into the same principal-agent problems you have with the Republican Party now? The far better solution is to organize the Conservative, Tea Party, Libertarian, and other activist wings of the Republican Party and begin to take it over from within. Starting at the local Republican

Committee level, many Libertarian groups have already had some success in doing this. Developing this bench of candidates from the bottom up will allow us to have a greater voice in the happenings of the national Republican Party structure. It is these people who nominate state chairpersons and committee persons, and they in turn nominate the national Republican Party Chairman.

Another reason to avoid a third-party movement is both tactical and mathematical. Even if you manage to build a rival party, rather than taking back the Republican Party you built, the simple electoral math is not in your favor. Primaries and nominating conventions for political office are largely dominated by the most dedicated voters, with the most passionate beliefs. What would likely happen would be the Democratic candidate would appeal to the wing of his party, which is dominated by far-left Liberals, knowing that he or she wouldn't need to move back toward the political center during the general election because the Republican vote would be split among the Republican Party and the new, third-party candidate. Making matters worse is that the true Conservative and Libertarian voters would be able to run and win their primary or convention as principled candidates, but the candidates running for the traditional Republican nomination would feel no need to run on these values. After all, they are going to be nominated by the people who remained registered as Republicans after the Conservatives and Libertarians splinter off and are only likely to be Conservative on a limited set of issues, which appeal to his or her now limited Republican voter base. We would be left with a weak Republican Party nominee splitting the vote with a Conservative or Libertarian nominee, and a Liberal likely winning the general election by a plurality of votes. The effects of this would be devastating as purple and even Republican red states would become hotbeds of Liberal organizational activity and activist and donor money in a get-out-the-vote effort looking to expand their base. With the media on their side, this is a recipe for disaster.

A more practical solution to the problem of spineless politicians hijacking the Republican Party banner and refusing to do anything to advance liberty and fiscal Conservatism is to "trade up." This strategy had been talked about within the activist movement for years and it has the potential to change not only the Republican Party, but the country, too. The trade-up strategy is based on the tenet that no Republican Party lawmaker should ever be considered "safe." The solemn duty of holding a political office is neither a game, nor an entitlement, and we must get away from the popularity contest atmosphere that has taken over the modern political ecosystem. The process should be a results-oriented business and the results a lawmaker produces are votes. If any Republican, in any office, regardless of his or her charisma, personal life story, good looks, or any other appealing characteristic outside of their voting history, votes against principles we stand for, then we should have a candidate waiting in the wings to primary him or her and trade up. Elected officials who do not fear a primary challenge grow comfortable taking votes, which are dictated more by their personal ambitions rather than the interests of the voters who elected them and the trade-up strategy, when credibly introduced, eliminates this sense of comfort and forces them to stick to principles or risk losing their job.

Some lawmakers would chasten us if we were to move toward this strategy nationwide largely because they don't want to be the ones primaried, and also because they'll say that it's a waste of precious campaign time and money to constantly have to allocate resources to "safe" Republican districts. Some would also be

uncomfortable with severing personal relationships they have
with other lawmakers if they decided to challenge their friends in
primaries, but these concerns are a small price to pay to take back
the party infrastructure we built. And, with regard to the "It's a
waste of campaign resources" tripe, that statement is nonsense. The
"waste" of resources would be largely offset over time with the
addition of resources from activated grassroots activists and donors
reengaging in the political process because they now have someone running for office who they believe in. Many of these people
have been dormant in the political process because they feel the
current two-party system forces them to choose between the "lesser
of two evils."

18

Are There Any Good Guys Left? Here's the Bad News

The political environment in Washington, DC, makes it easy to pick out the various bad apples responsible for destroying the sacred citizen-legislator relationship, but are there any good guys left? After working behind the scenes as a Secret Service agent in three presidential campaigns and Hillary Clinton's New York State Senate campaign, along with my own campaigns for the U.S. Senate and House of Representatives, I must report, regretfully, that there are very few good guys left. I met with a number of elected officials during my political campaigns and was almost always disappointed. The smug air of arrogance and the dismissive nature of their questions nearly always left me with a deep sense of disappointment as I would walk back to my car after those meetings. Although the origins of the phrase are mysterious, the words, "Washington is Hollywood for ugly people" never appeared more true during those walks. I was reminded of this phrase in February 2015 when reading a *Daily Caller* piece by Patrick Howley entitled "Romney Aide: Axelrod LIED About What Mitt Said to Obama on

Concession Call."* The piece refutes former Obama administration insider and adviser David Axelrod's allegation in his book that during Republican Party presidential nominee Mitt Romney's concession call to President Obama, he said, "You really did a great job of getting the vote out in places like Cleveland and Milwaukee." Axelrod subsequently stated that the now reelected President Obama thought that Romney was referring to "black people." Although I obviously was not there for the concession phone call, I am inclined to believe the recount of the moment as told to Patrick Howley by former Romney aide Garrett Jackson who stated in *The Daily Caller* piece, "It was totally absurd. I know it didn't happen because I was right next to him there. Hell, I was the one who called the president on my phone." I believe Garret Jackson because David Axelrod, in my experience, lacks the moral compass to distinguish between rough politics and truly dirty politics. I have very real doubts that Mitt Romney ever uttered those words and that Axelrod was simply trying to sell books, something I know a lot about considering the money I could have made if I decided to tell salacious, behind-the-scenes stories about the Obama administration. Tarring the reputation of a dignified man such as Romney with a racially tinged insult, "conveniently" timed during the beginning of the 2016 presidential election cycle, and to sell books written on a bed of lies, is just the type of thing David Axelrod does. Between allegations of pushing trashy stories about the personal lives of Republican and Democratic opponents and other allegations of leaking divorce records, David Axelrod is the embodiment of nearly everything that is wrong with Washington,

*Patrick Howley, "Romney Aide: Axelrod LIED About What Mitt Said to Obama on Concession Call," *Daily Caller*, February 4, 2015, dailycaller.com/2015/02/04/romney-aide-axelrod-lied-about-what-mitt-said-to-obama-on-concession-call/.

DC—personal ambitions overriding an ambition to change the country for the better.

As with any rule though, there are always exceptions and thankfully, there are exceptions to the maxim that all of our elected representatives have sold us out. A small number of U.S. senators and congressmen supported me both behind the scenes and publicly despite the long odds, and I am convinced that they did so because of their allegiance to the Conservative cause. There was no quid pro quo possible for their support because I had nothing to offer them in return, nor would I offer any payback as a matter of principle.

It's sad that there are so few elected officials in Washington, DC, willing to play "the long game" for America's future. With all of the pressures and corrupting influences on the elected insiders in Washington, DC, it's disappointing, but unsurprising, that so many fail the leadership tests. Working as a Secret Service agent during the negotiations and lead-up to the Obamacare legislation was an eye-opening experience for me. From the perspective of an "outsider" on the "inside" it appeared that everyone had a say in the design of Obamacare, with the exception of the people that mattered, all of us. Watching the endless parade of lobbyists, connected insiders, corrupted academics, crony business leaders, headline-seeking politicians, messaging gurus, speechwriters, bought-and-sold politicians, and left-wing ideologues meet with the President and his staff, made me question if any of these people had considered the original Hippocratic Oath, specifically the portion that states "according to my judgment and means; and I will take care that they suffer no hurt or damage," before they upended the entire U.S. healthcare system?

Watching this debacle unfold also reminded me that it's not just politicians who are selling out the country's future, but the legions of others seeking favors from the government, at the expense of others, while either lecturing us about the perils of concentrated power in the corporate sector or about the dangers of "big money" in politics. The hypocrisy is nearly unbearable to watch from behind the curtain in Washington, DC, as many of the stories we've been told are dismantled one by one by the reality that many of the people and groups we believed in are just fairy tales. Many of these people and groups do their best to continue to ensure that there are no good people left in the Washington, DC, bubble by using their money and their followings as chips in a game of political poker where your liberty and freedom are at stake.

19

Hillary's E-mails, Sebelius' Politicking, and Clapper's Lies

One needs to look no further than at the hubris of former First Lady and Secretary of State Hillary Clinton for an example of what's good for the gander being ignored by the goose. Both former President Bill Clinton and Hillary Clinton, with their deep ties to elected officials, the bureaucracy, connected crony capitalists, lobbyists, foreign governments, moneyed interests, and Washington, DC, influence peddlers, are textbook examples of the new government ruling class. They have spent their life's work building a network to ensure their perpetual influence and seat at the table when the big decisions are made. Access to the Clintons is access to the gates of power, and the ability to bypass all of the traditional rules that the rest of us are forced to live under. They shamefully skirt the rules, which they lecture us about and, although they sometimes suffer short-term media backlash, they rarely suffer any long-term consequences. It is infuriating to me, and many others both inside and outside of the government, that Hillary Clinton used a private e-mail server to conduct the official business of the American people and still trots out her surrogates (i.e., Lanny Davis, James Carville) with no shame to defend this egregious breach of rules, ethics, and protocol. I recall as a Secret Service agent very strict rules on information security and e-mail procedures that any government employee handling sensitive information would be familiar with. Without delving deeply into those rules, it was clear to anyone working with us that personal e-mail accounts were strictly forbidden for handling sensitive data and information. It strains credulity and borders on absurdity to believe that Hillary Clinton conducted *all* of her official business on her own personal e-mail server, away from the custody of the American people, and never sent *any* classified or sensitive information over that system. I am aware of sources, who fear coming forward, who know that the Clinton machine is not telling the whole e-mail scandal story. I remember being on a foreign protection mission as an agent, when computer thumb drives first became ubiquitous, and watching a supervisory agent sweat out a work schedule deadline he was going to miss because he refused to put the work schedule on an unsecured, personal thumb drive. E-mail wasn't working properly on the trip and he had no way to transfer the work schedule electronically without printing it and typing the entire document over again and, although there were no formal rules on thumb drives at that time, he just knew it was a bad idea to use that thumb drive. He didn't need a government rule book to tell him that sending information over an unsecured network, in a foreign country, unencrypted, was a bad idea. Judging by Hillary Clinton's actions she doesn't care about either the formal or informal rules, or what the average government employee would judge as a good or bad idea. Hillary is an educated woman and she must have known that this was, at a minimum, a violation of the spirit of the federal rules restricting the use of private e-mail accounts for official government business. The point is that she likely didn't care. She is part of the benighted class that has managed to leverage their power and their reputations for smearing and destroying anyone getting in their way, into a "public service" career that is really a public, get-rich-quick sham.

It's the informal rules, which the Clinton's have managed to bypass as well. During my run for the sixth congressional district seat in Congress in the 2014 election cycle, I did not reside in the district I ran. I never hid that fact and was honest about my desire to represent the district in the U.S. House of Representatives, but I was still attacked by many on the Left as a "carpetbagger." I understand why they would do so because politics is a dirty game, but I often wondered how many of those people were Clinton acolytes. I was at the Clinton residence when the moving van showed up and delivered many of her personal items long after she declared her intention to be a U.S. senator in New York. She lived there, and spent time there before election night, but it was obvious to anyone on the inside that she was no New Yorker. The press largely gave her a pass on this after some short-term ribbing, but it was another example of the "Teflon Clintons" as the long-term damage was nil. The Clintons flaunting their ability to bypass the formal and informal rules must be frustrating to the federal officials and bureaucrats that have worked for them. How is it that Secret Service agents couldn't discuss over personal e-mail the means by which we would sacrifice our security, to ensure hers, over a private server without the threat of being terminated or prosecuted, but she could sacrifice our entire nation's security, and potentially correspond with the White House while doing it, without a perceived penalty?

The Clintons' use and misuse of our taxpayer-funded federal

government for personal advancement was not limited to Hillary Clinton's e-mail practices. There have also been inquiries into her ability to get allies hired in important positions of influence within our government, without them having to forfeit their private-sector employment. She accomplished this by requesting that they be granted "special government employee" status for these allies. Although this is not unprecedented, it does fit with a pattern of secrecy by the Clintons and invited questions because, according to Senator Charles Grassley in an interview with Tom Hamburger of *The Washington Post*, "Others, Grassley said, appeared to have turned the program on its head: Instead of being outside experts brought in to assist the government, they were State Department employees who launched secondary careers in the private sector while remaining tied to the department."* Can you fathom a scenario where a Secret Service agent would be allowed to retain his job while providing private-sector security consulting for a foreign government? Again, what's good for the Clintons is not good for the many people who support them from an administrative, security, and political perspective. Any agent who engaged in this type of behavior would be terminated and likely prosecuted while the person they protect is actively engaging in, or sanctioning, the same behavior.

Hillary Clinton is not the only member of the new government ruling class who lives by a different, and more accommodating set of rules than the rest of us. Connected Obama administration insider and Director of National Intelligence James Clapper is another

---

*Tom Hamburger, "Clinton emails reinvigorate inquiry into allies who got special job status," *Washington Post*, March 9, 2015, www.washingtonpost.com/politics/clinton-e -mails-prompt-another-inquiry-on-capitol-hill/2015/03/09/db3cd3b4-c374-11e4-9ec2 -b418f57a4a99_story.html?wpisrc=nl_evening&wpmm=1.

member. On March 12, 2013, Senator Ron Wyden asked Clapper whether intelligence officials collect data on American citizens. Clapper, in another act of ruling-class hubris, responded, "No, sir," and, "Not wittingly. There are cases where they could inadvertently perhaps collect, but not wittingly."* There are only two possible scenarios for this and the first is unlikely. Either Clapper was unaware of the NSA's massive metadata-collection efforts, which ensnared American citizens, or Clapper knew about the program and lied to the senator with little fear of being caught. Regardless of where you may personally stand on the data-collection efforts of the NSA, I can assure you that a lie of this magnitude, in front of the Senate Intelligence Committee would end the career of any other federal employee not included in the ruling class. As for Clapper he submitted a letter "explaining" his false testimony and never suffered any more than a few days of negative media attention because he was a member of the insider class.

Another deeply personal example of the sins of the ruling class being broadly forgiven while everyone else is lorded over by insider hypocrites, involves a brazen abuse of the Hatch Act by former Health and Human Services Secretary Kathleen Sebelius in February 2012. This example hits home because I had to resign from the job I loved as a Secret Service agent in order to fight for a political cause I believed in because of the Hatch Act restrictions against political activity. Secret Service agents fall under the most restricted Hatch Act categories, which prohibit political activities while employed as an agent. Outside of placing a bumper sticker

---

*Glenn Kessler, "Clapper's 'least untruthful' statement to the Senate." *Washington Post*, June 12, 2013, www.washingtonpost.com/blogs/fact-checker/post/james-clappers-least -untruthful-statement-to-the-senate/2013/06/11/e50677a8-d2d8-11e2-a73e -826d299ff459_blog.html.

on my car, I was generally prohibited from volunteering on a campaign, endorsing a candidate, and most other political activities of consequence. I abided by the letter of the law and the spirit of the law and, even as I yearned to do more to help course correct the path we were on as a country, I had had to stand on the sideline and painfully observe. I remember driving to get gas in my car one afternoon, a few months before the 2010 elections, and seeing now Congressman Andy Harris, then-candidate Andy Harris, waving his campaign signs on a hot and sticky summer day, with a rather large and boisterous team of supporters on the corner of an major intersection. Their uncoordinated movements ranged from waving signs to dancing to waving to jumping up and down, but we all got the message. I felt their passion and desperately wanted to be a part of it. There's a yearning in all of us to be part of collective group of people all sharing a similar cause. Most of us would rather be together and fighting for a cause, rather than alone and in peace. I wanted in and I couldn't, and it hurt. I simply drove by, rolled down my window, and yelled, "Go get 'em!" and, disappointed, I drove home. Well, Kathleen Sebelius never drove home. Sebelius decided it would be easier to ignore the rules the rest of us live by and, during a Human Rights Campaign Gala Dinner in North Carolina, began actively campaigning for Barack Obama's reelection when, while acting in her official capacity, she said, "It's hugely important to make sure that we re-elect the president and elect a Democratic governor here in North Carolina."* Was Sebelius punished? Only if your version of punishment is a token investigation where Secretary Sebelius admitted the trip was political and de-

---

*Paige Winfield Cunningham, "Pro-Obama speech ruled Hatch Act violation; Sebelius repays travel costs." *Washington Times*, September 12, 2012, www.washingtontimes.com/news/2012/sep/12/sebelius-unlawfully-stumped-for-obama/.

cided to personally pay for the trip. I would have been given no such leniency, and neither would you.

The real tragedy here is that the new government ruling class will continue to infect our government until big and bold changes are made. Why are public officials, granted enormous powers by the citizens of the United States, held to a lower, and not higher, standard of conduct? Why are we punished under a system of rules and regulations, while the people we expect to provide principled leadership escape the rules and the punishments for violating them? None of this will change until we collectively push for harsher, not more lenient punishment for public servants who violate our trust. Having been both a police officer and a federal agent I can attest to the power of handcuffs. It may appear harsh, but the loss of freedom is the only thing that will change this type of ruling-class behavior. There is a near magical power to handcuffs and the deterrent effect of seeing one of your colleagues in them. The ruling class has grown in power and, until we harshly prosecute one of them and make them suffer the indignities of the loss of prestige that comes with arrest, they will continue to accurately forecast that violating the rules pays off because they will not be punished.

20

America Needs to "Get Big"

In the new America President Obama has created, through his pledge to "fundamentally transform" the country, liberty is under attack. In the six years of the Obama presidency we have seen his newly created Consumer Financial Protection Bureau wage a de facto economic war through fines, and economic extortion, against for-profit educational institutions, the auto loan industry, the financial industry, and consumer privacy. We have witnessed the IRS potentially alter the course of a presidential election by selectively targeting the President's political opponents for government harassment during a critical organizing period for a presidential election. We have witnessed the President of the United States, the unquestioned leader of the free world, inject the power of the White House bully pulpit into extremely sensitive, and ongoing, local police use-of-force incidents and fan the flames of racial division in the country in a cynical effort to leverage division for personal political gain. We have seen an administration disregard the fundamental constitutional provisions of separation of powers and checks and balances on concentrated government power in order to devalue American citizenship and erase national definable borders. We have seen a President engage in persistent, disingenuous class-warfare rhetoric in a misguided attempt to siphon more tax dollars from the wallets of struggling Americans, despite the fact that the government is collecting historic amounts of tax revenue from its citizens. We have seen an administration hijack our entire national healthcare system using unparalleled parliamentary trickery to jam through a historically unpopular healthcare law and then demonstrate epic incompetence while failing to even launch a Web site for the program. We have been subjected to a complete lockdown of the U.S. Senate under Harry Reid to ensure that an already paid for nuclear waste facility in his state never receives any nuclear waste. We have a Department of Justice, which refuses to prosecute an IRS official who played a central role in the targeting of innocent Americans and drops an open-and-shut voter-intimidation case against a group of men standing outside of a polling location with clubs because both cases run counter to the "narrative" they want all of us to believe. We have an administration, which is perfectly comfortable lying about the circumstances that led to the release of Bowe Bergdahl, the deaths of four American patriots in the special mission complex in Benghazi, the failed Fast and Furious gun-running operation, and the targeting of journalists at both the Associated Press and Fox News. And, finally, we have an administration that has disrespected everything this country stands for while trampling on the honor of the brave souls who gave their lives to preserve the God-given freedoms that have been protected by our peerless system of government for more than two hundred years.

Now, here is the good news. It's time for America to "get big." During my Secret Service training program I was trained and retrained to "get big." "Get big" was a Secret Service term for making yourself as big of a target as possible in the event that shots are fired at the President. This mechanically simple act runs counter to every psychological and evolutionary impulse human beings possess. It is a basic human reflex to duck when something is thrown at you, to put your hands up when something is headed toward your face, and to get out of the way if bullets are flying in your direction. Training a Secret Service agent to "get big" is extremely difficult because thousands of repetitions in training exercises are required before you can unlearn how to be human, and relearn how to be a human shield. If you care to see what "get big" looks like in action, then watch the video of Secret Service agent Tim McCarthy being shot in 1981. McCarthy was shot because the shooter, John Hinckley Jr., fired at President Ronald Reagan. But Agent McCarthy got big for the American people at the exact moment they needed him to. McCarthy was not going to allow the President to be attacked without him getting in the way, not on that day, not on his watch. McCarthy takes that bullet like a true American hero while turning toward it and spreading himself out to become as big a target as possible. We have reached a point in our history where the American people are all going to have to "get big" in their own small ways in order to save our country.

All of us are going to have to sacrifice something to fix what has been broken, but those short-term sacrifices will secure a future of unimaginable prosperity if we can collectively move past our differences. This country is bigger than Barack Obama, it's bigger than many of its failed Republican leaders, and it's bigger than the legions of bureaucrats and elected officials who prance around Washington, DC, with their noses in their air thinking that they've beat the system when, all the while, the American people were taking notes and keeping score. The jig is up. The rebirth of grassroots politics with the Tea Party rebellion, when combined with innovations in voter targeting, voter data, and a new era of candidates able to bypass the traditional Washington, DC, gate-keepers and speak directly to the people, has the potential to lead us to a path to a better tomorrow. The explosive growth in materials science, medical technology, supply-chain technologies, business management, risk management, information technology, sanitation technology, educational delivery methods, and government ac-countability through the geometric growth of new media, all have the potential to lead us down the road to a future where today's measures of wealth are tomorrow's floor, not its ceiling. This will require work and sacrifice though. We will have to accept a personal commitment to "do." It's the "do" that matters, not the talk. When I walked away from certain financial security and a future in a job I loved with the U.S. Secret Service to fight the good fight, I knew that my small sacrifice paled in comparison to the sacrifices made by our fighting men and women to preserve our Republic, but it was my way of fighting back. Find your way. Find a group to join or find a campaign to volunteer for, or a cause to fight for. Go find your fight and, when that problem comes your way, don't duck, Get big.

INDEX